The Interpreter

Chinese

Foreign Languages Press

First Edition **2007**
Second Printing **2008**

Editor: Yan Jing
English Editor: Xu Rong
Editorial Assistant: Fred Richardson

ISBN 978-7-119-04792-8

Copyright ©2007 Lydia Chen
Published by Foreign Languages Press
24 Baiwanzhuang Road, Beijing 100037, China
http://www.flp.com.cn
Distributed by China International Book Trading Corporation
35 Chegongzhuang Xilu, Beijing 100044, China
P.O. Box 399, Beijing, China

Printed in the People's Republic of China

Contents

Introduction

Pronunciation Guide

1: Essentials   **1**

22 Sentence Patterns   2
Self-introduction   4
Courtesies   4
Key Phrases   4
Bridging the Gap   6
Emergencies   6
Signs   8

2: Travel   **9**

Asking for Information   10
Identification   10
Booking a Ticket   10
Waiting to Board   12
All Aboard   14
Baggage Claim   16
Customs   16
Signs   18

3: Local Transport   **19**

Getting Set   20
Taking a Taxi   20
Hiring a Car   22
Going by Bus   24
Riding the Subway   24
On Foot   26
Renting a Bike   26
Signs   28

4: Hotel   **29**

Checking In   30
Checking Out   30
Service Inquiries   32
Problems in the Room   34
Housekeeping   34
Laundry   36
Making a Phone Call   36
The Foreign Exchange Desk   38
The Post Office   40
Faxes   42
The Barbershop   42
Signs   44

5: Friends   **45**

Opening Lines   46
Talk About the Weather   46
Talk About Family   48
Talk About Work   48
Talk About Hobbies   48
Talk About Politics   50
Saying Good-bye   50
Signs   52

6: Food   **53**

Eating on the Run   54
Finding a Place to Eat   54
Making Reservations   56
Getting a Table   56
Ordering   58
During the Meal   60
Ending the Meal   60
Signs   62

7: Sightseeing   **63**

Planning Your Excursion   64
At the Sight   64
At the Zoo   66
At the Factory   66
Taking a Photo   68
Signs   70

8: Shopping   **71**

Scouting the Market   72
Making the Find   72
Closing the Deal   74
Art and Antiques   74
Books   74
Clothing   76
Film   76
Returns and Repairs   78
Signs   80

9: Entertainment   **81**

Choosing a Show   82
Buying Tickets   82
Getting Seated   82
Asking for Background   84
Showing Appreciation   84
Signs   86

10: Health   **87**

Getting Help   88
Complaints   88
Requests   88
Questions   90
Taking Leave   90

Dentist   90
Signs   92

English-Chinese Dictionary   **93**
Chinese-English Supplement   **179**
Appendices   **201**

A: Numbers and Quantities   **201**
Cardinal Numbers   201
Ordinal Numbers   202
Fractions   202
Percentages   202

B: Measure Words   **203**

C: Expressions of Time   **205**

D: Conversion Charts   **206**
Measures   206
Temperature   207

E: Money   **208**
Chinese Currency   208
Foreign Currencies   208

F: Place Names   **209**
Major Administrative Divisions   209
Cities of Interest   210

G: Dynasties   **212**

H: Family Relations   **213**

I: Useful Telephone Numbers   **215**

SIDEBARS

1: Essentials

No Verb Conjugations	3
Where? There!	3
Negatives	3
Questions	5
Measure Words	5
Past Tense	7
Zheige or Zhege?	7
What You'll Hear	7

2: Travel

International Airlines	11
What Kind of Plane Is This?	13
Good, Better, Best	15
The Best in Life	15
Good-byes	17
What You'll Hear	17

3: Local Transport

Which Way Is North?	21
Taxi Fares	21
Bus Numbers	23
Riding Public Buses	23
Bus Stops	25
Bicycle	27
What You'll Hear	27

4: Hotel

Local Hostels	31
Chinese Zodiac	31
Long-distance Communications	33
English-language Publications	35
Chinese-language Newspapers	37
Post Office Tips	39
Tea	41
Batteries	43

What You'll Hear	43

5: Friends

Chinese Names	47
(Psst... What'll I call Him?)	47
Chinese Idioms	49
Seeing Off a Friend	51
What You'll Hear	51

6: Food

What's for Breakfast?	55
What's for Dinner?	57
Local Snacks	59
What You'll Hear	61

7: Sightseeing

Symbols	65
Flowers	65
Trees	67
Zoo Animals	69
What You'll Hear	69

8: Shopping

Cashier's Booth	73
Special Items	73
Buying Jade	75
How to Bargain	77
Renminbi	79
What You'll Hear	79

9: Entertainment

Musical Instruments	83
Chinese Operas	83
What You'll Hear	85

10: Health

Where Does It Hurt?	89
Doctor, I Have...	89
What You'll Hear	91

Introduction

Going to China is a dream come true for many Westerners. The opportunities for business, vacation, and educational trips are common. Without some knowledge of the Chinese language, however, you will find yourself either confined to hotels and offices where English is spoken, or totally dependent on the services of an interpreter. To help you have some independence while in China, *The Pocket Interpreter: Chinese* provides the sentence patterns you will most often need and the vocabulary with which you can create new sentences. In addition, each chapter includes brief information which will help you better understand the Chinese people, their society, and their culture.

The design of this book is to offer basic sentences upon which other sentences can be patterned, rather than attempt to provide specific phrases for every situation the China traveler could possibly encounter. You can use this book effectively by mastering the basic patterns, such as "... *zài nǎr*?" (Where is...?) and "*Yǒu méi yǒu*... ?" (Do you have...?), and referring to the dictionary for the specific words you need to make the sentence you want. The twenty-two sentence patterns introduced in Chapter One recur often in the subsequent chapters. By recognizing the patterns each time they reappear, you will soon be able to use them on your own.

In the patterns, the words for which substitutions can be made have been bracketed in both the English and Chinese pinyin versions. Thus you will know where to replace a given word with one that is more suited to your needs. For example, if the English sentence is "Where is the (zoo)?" the corresponding Chinese would be "(*Dòngwùyuán*) *zài nǎr*?" Seeing that *dòngwùyuán* is the equivalent of zoo, you could then look up another word in the dictionary, such as museum, and substitute its Chinese equivalent, *bówùguǎn*, in the given sentence. "Where is the museum?" would thus be "*Bówùguǎn zài nǎr*?"

The Chinese words in this book have been spelled according to the pinyin system, the official transliteration of Putonghua used in the People's Republic of China. Putonghua, or Modern Standard Chinese (MSC), also commonly called Mandarin, is the national language of China. Taking Beijing dialect as the basic pronunciation and based on northern dialects, it is used in national broadcasts and taught in public schools throughout China. When among people of their own locality, however, Chinese still speak their own local dialects, which vary greatly from region to region. In Guangzhou, for example, you will hear people around you speaking Cantonese, which bears almost no resemblance to Putonghua. Nevertheless, Putonghua is generally understood and you can use it wherever you go in China.

Since most Chinese do not read pinyin easily, the phrases here are also given in Chinese characters, or *Hànzì*. The *Hànzì* used are the simplified Chinese characters, which are slightly different from the traditional characters used in Taiwan, Hong Kong, Singapore, and other places. People who know the traditional characters can usually figure out the simplified forms by context. If you have difficulty pronouncing a Chinese word or phrase, you can point to the accompanying *Hànzì* and ask the Chinese with whom you wish to communicate to read it.

Every Chinese written character represents a one-syllable word. Many Chinese words, however, are compounds composed of two or more characters which each contribute meaning to the total concept. For example, the word for movie is *diànyǐng* (电影), composed of the words *diàn* (electric) and *yǐng* (shadow). For ease of reading, the two syllables have been spelled together as one word in pinyin; in *Hànzì* they are two separate characters.

In Putonghua, each syllable is composed of an initial sound, a final sound, and a tone. (*See Pronunciation Guide*) The word *diàn*, for example, has the initial sound *d*, the final sound *ian*, and the downward fourth tone (`). You will notice that some words in pinyin do not have tonal marks above them. This is because they are unstressed syllables which should be spoken quickly in a neutral tone.

A few words, such as *yī* (one), are not always marked with the same tone when they appear in different phrases. This is because the tone of some words depends on the tone of the word following it. *Yī*, for example, should only be spoken in the first tone when it stands alone or is followed by a pause; if the next word is a first-, second-, or third-tone word, *yī* should be read as *yì*; if the next word is a fourth-tone word, *yī* should be read as *yí*. Similarly *bù* (not) should be read as *bú* when the word following it is a fourth-tone word. For convenience, *yī* and *bù* have been marked in this book according to the tones in which they should be read within the phrase given, not as they are listed in the dictionary.

The tone, or inflection, of a Chinese word is just as important as its pronunciation. This aspect of speaking Chinese is the most difficult for English speakers to learn. In English, the tone of a word varies with the mood of the sentence; in Chinese, the tone stays the same whether the sentence is a question, exclamation, or matter-of-fact statement. Mood is indicated by stress on certain words, rather than inflection. To use the wrong tone in a Chinese word would be the equivalent of saying "cat" for "dog" in English.

The key to learning a new language is repetition. Begin by practicing a few simple phrases, such as _nǐhǎo_ (hello) and _xièxie_ (thank you), which you can use many times a day. Then build up to the useful phrases presented in Chapter One. To perfect your Putonghua, ask a Chinese friend to help you with your pronunciations and tones. Also, reinforce your grasp of the language by listening and looking. Be on the alert for the commonly heard phrases and often seen signs presented at the end of each chapter. With these thoughts in mind, a positive outlook, and book in hand, _Yílùshùnfēng_ (may good winds follow you)!

Pronunciation Guide

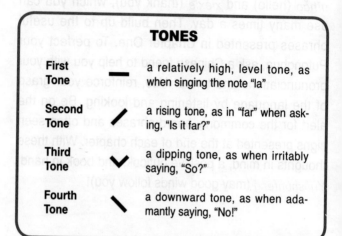

TONES

First Tone	—	a relatively high, level tone, as when singing the note "la"
Second Tone	/	a rising tone, as in "far" when asking, "Is it far?"
Third Tone	∨	a dipping tone, as when irritably saying, "So?"
Fourth Tone	\	a downward tone, as when adamantly saying, "No!"

INITIAL SOUNDS

b, d, f, g, h, j, k, l, m, n, p, s, t, w, y	roughly the same as in English
ch, sh	as in English, but curl the tongue up toward the roof of the mouth while pronouncing the "ch" or "sh" sound
c	ts as in cats
q	ch as in cheese
r	zhr, like in pleasure
x	sh as in banshee
z	ds as in cards
zh	dg as in fudge

FINAL SOUNDS

a	ah
ai	eye
an	ahn
ang	ahng
ao	ow
ar	are
e	uh
ei	eigh as in a sleigh
en	un as in run
eng	ung as in hung
er	cross between ar and er
i	ee, but after c, ch, r, s, sh, z, and zh it is silent
ia	ee-ah (quickly, as one syllable)
ian	ee-en (quickly)
iang	ee-ahng (quickly)
iao	ee-ow (quickly)
ie	ee-eh (quickly)
in	een as in seen
ing	ing as in ring
iong	ee-ōng (quickly)
iu	eo as in Leo
o	o as in or
ong	ōng
ou	oh
u	oo as in moo
ü	cross between oo and eew, as in French tu
ua	wa as in wash
uai	why
uan	wahn, as in wander
uang	wahng
ue	weh
ui	way
un	won
uo	wo as in wore

1 Essentials

Méi bànfǎ.
Tough luck
(there's no other way)

How do you even begin to learn Chinese? When you arrive in China, you will find yourself suddenly the "foreigner." At first you may feel at a loss, not knowing what to say. Gradually, by learning a few essentials, you will find your new surroundings less formidable. The sentence patterns and phrases introduced here are the ones you will draw upon most often in your travels. Master these, and you'll be able to tackle China on your own.

22 Sentence Patterns

Can I (enter)?	*Wǒ néng bù néng (jìnqu) ?*
Can you (help me)?	*Nǐ néng bù néng (bāngmáng) ?*
Do you have (postcards)?	*Yǒu (míngxìnpiàn) ma?*
How much does (this) cost?	*(Zhèige) yào duōshao qián?*
I am (American).	*Wǒ shì (Měiguórén).*
I am not (a movie star).	*Wǒ bú shì (diànyǐng míngxīng).*
I have (two pieces of luggage).	*Wǒ yǒu (liǎng jiàn xíngli).*
I do not have (a map).	*Wǒ méi yǒu (dìtú).*
I lost my (passport).	*Wǒde (hùzhào) diū le.*
I need (to see a doctor),	*Wǒ yào (kànbìng).*
I do not need (a taxi).	*Wǒ bú yào (chūzūchē).*
I would like to (go to the zoo).	*Wǒ xiǎng (qù dòngwùyuán).*
I would not like to (rest).	*Wǒ bùxiǎng (xiūxi).*
I will stay in (Beijing) for [three days].	*Wǒ yào zài (Běijīng) dāi [sāntiān].*
Is there a (restaurant) nearby?	*Fùjìn yǒu (fànguǎn) ma?*
Please give me (a receipt).	*Qǐng gěi wǒ (fāpiào).*
Please help me (register).	*Qǐ bāng wǒ (dēngjì).*
This is my (shoulder bag).	*Zhè shì wǒde (bēibāo).*
This is not my (camera).	*Zhè bú shì wǒde (zhàoxiàngjī).*
When does (the bank) open?	*(Yíháng) shénme shíhou kāimén?*
Where can I find (coffee)?	*Nǎr yǒu (kāfēi)?*
Where is (the post office)?	*(Yóujú) zài nǎr?*

我能不能进去?

你能不能帮忙?

有明信片吗?

这个要多少钱?

我是美国人。

我不是电影明星。

我有两件行李。

我没有地图。

我的护照丢了。

我要看病。

我不要出租车。

我想去动物园。

我不想休息。

我要在北京呆三天。

附近有饭馆吗?

请给我发票。

请帮我登记。

这是我的背包。

这不是我的照相机。

银行什么时候开门?

哪儿有咖啡?

邮局在哪儿?

No Verb Conjugations

The easy part of learning Chinese is that there are no verb conjugations. I, you, he, we, and they, all take the same verb form. For example:

I am	*wǒ shì*
You are	*Nǐ shì*
He is	*Tā shì*
We are	*Wǒmen shì*
You are (pl)	*Nǐmen shì*
They are	*Tāmen shì*

The pronouns are also easy to remember. The plural forms are the singular forms plus the syllable *men* (们).

Where? There!

You will find that people from different regions in China prefer different words to express the same idea, and Putonghua incorporates these varia. For example, *nǎr* and *nǎli* both mean "where" and *nàr* and *nàli*, likewise, mean "there". People in the north tend to prefer the "r" sound, as in *nǎr*, whereas southerners prefer a crisper sound, as in *nǎli*.

Negatives

The negative form of most verbs in Chinese is formed by adding the syllable *bù* (不) before the verb, almost like the word "not" in English. For example:

I know.	*wǒ zhīdao.*
I don't know.	*wǒ bù zhīdao.*

However, with the verb *yǒu* (to have), the negative is formed with the syllable *méi* (没).

He has money.	*Tā yǒu qián.*
He doesn't have money.	*Tā méi yǒu qián.*

ESSENTIALS

Self-introduction

Hello.	Nǐhǎo.
My name is (John Smith).	Wǒ jiào (John Smith).
My last name is (Smith).	Wǒ xìng (Smith).
We're a group of (five).	Wǒmen gòng yǒu (wǔ) gè rén.
We're with (XYZ Company)	Wǒmen shì (XYZ gōngsī) de.

Courtesies

May I have your last name, please?	Nín guì xìng?
Thank you.	Xièxie.
You're welcome.	Bú kèqi.
Sorry.	Duìbuqǐ.
I'm so sorry.	Zhēn duìbuqǐ.
It's nothing.	Méi guānxi.
Excuse me (may I trouble you)...	Máfán nǐ...
Excuse me (may I ask)...	Qǐng wèn...
Excuse me (sorry).	Duìbuqǐ.
Excuse me (make way, hate to disturb you)...	Láojià...
I'm leaving now. Bye!	Wǒ zǒu le. Zàijiàn!

Key Phrases

What's this?	Zhè shì shénme?
Which one?	Nǎige?
This one.	Zhèige.

你好!

我叫 John Smith.

我姓 Smith.

我们共有五个人。

我们是 XYZ 公司的。

您贵姓?

谢谢。

不客气。

对不起。

真对不起!

没关系。

麻烦你……

请问……

对不起。

劳驾……

我走了，再见!

这是什么?

哪个?

这个。

Questions

Questions are formed in Chinese by adding the syllable *ma* (吗) at the end of a statement or by inserting the negative form of a verb or modifier immediately after that verb or modifier. For example:

He is your friend.
Tā shì nǐde péngyǒu.
Is he your friend?
Tā shì nǐde péngyǒu ma?
Is he (or is he not) your friend?
Tā shì bú shì nǐde péngyǒu?

Measure Words

One of the most difficult skills in Chinese is the use of measure words. Every noun has a specific measure word that is used to count or refer to it, just like "gaggle" refers to geese and "pride" refers to lions in English.

The generic measure word in Chinese is *gè* (个) which can refer to almost anything. However, use of specific measure words is more proper. The proper measure word for books, for example, is *běn* (tome or edition). Whenever books are mentioned, *běn* precedes *shū* (book):

one book   *yì běn shū*
this book   *zhèi běn shū*
five book   *wǔ běn shū*
which book?   *něi běn shū?*

For a list of common measure words, refer to Appendix B on page 203.

ESSENTIALS

That one.	Nèige.
Right.	Duì.
Wrong.	Bú duì.
Enough.	Gòu le.
Just right.	Zhèng hǎo.
How far?	Duōyuǎn?
How long (duration)?	Duōjiǔ?
How much?	Duōshao?
What time is it?	Xiànzài jǐdiǎn le?

Bridging the Gap

I don't understand.	Wǒ bù míngbái.
Please speak more slowly.	Qǐng shuō de màn yìdiǎn.
Please point to it.	Qǐng zhǐ gěi wǒ kàn.
Will you please repeat that?	Qǐng chóng fù yí biàn.
Could you write it down?	Nǐ néng xiě xià lái ma?
How do you pronounce this?	Zhèige zěnme niàn?
What does this mean?	Zhè shì shénme yìsi?

Emergencies

Help!	Jiù Mìng!
Call the police.	Kuài jiào jǐngchá.
Get a doctor.	Kuài jiào yīshēng lái.
There's a fire.	Nà biān qǐhuǒ le.
There's been an accident.	Nà biān chūshì le.
I've been robbed.	Wǒ bèi rén qiǎng le.
They took my...	Tā mén qiǎng le wǒ de...
I've lost my...	Wǒ diūle...
I'm lost.	Wǒ mílù le.
Watch out!	Xiǎo xīn!
Go Away!	Zǒu kāi (zǒu, zǒu, zǒu)!

6

那个。

对。

不对。

够了。

正好。

多远?

多久?

多少?

现在几点了?

我不明白。

请说得慢一点。

请指给我看。

请重复一遍。

你能写下来吗?

这个怎么念?

这是什么意思?

救命!

快叫警察。

快叫医生来。

那边着火了。

那边出事了。

我被人抢了。

他们抢了我的……

我丢了……

我迷路了。

小心!

走开!

Past Tense

The past tense of a verb in Chinese is made by adding the syllable *le* (了) immediately after the verb or at the very end of the sentence, For example:

I' m going.	*Wǒ qù*
I went.	*Wǒ qù le.*
I went shopping.	*Wǒ qù mǎi dōngxi le.*

Zheige or Zhege?

You might wonder why there is an inconsistency in the pronunciation, and pinyin spelling, of *zhè* (这), meaning "this"; *nà* (那), meaning "that"; and *nǎ* (哪), meaning "which." When the word following these indicators is a measure word, then *zhè* is often pronounced *zhèi*; *nà* is pronounced *nèi* or *nè*; and *nǎ* is pronounced *něi*. For example:

this one	*zhège, zhèige*
that one	*nàge, nèige, nège*
Which one?	*nǎge? něige?*

What You' ll Hear

bù hǎo	no good
bù xíng	not okay; doesn't work
děng yì děng	wait a while
hǎo	good
kě yǐ	can be done
Méi bànfǎ.	There's no solution.
Méi yǒu.	There isn't any.
Qǐng jìn.	Please come in.
xíng	okay
Wèi!	Hello. Hey!

Signs

rùkǒu
Entrance

chūkǒu
Exit

nán cèsuǒ
Men's Toilets

nǚ cèsuǒ
Women's Toilets

gōngyòng diànhuà
Public Telephone

8

èr 2 Travel

Yí lù shùnfēng!
Bon voyage
(good winds all the way)!

Traveling around China is fun. Making your own arrangements for travel, or being delayed in an airport or train station for several hours, however, can be another story. At those times, good communication is necessary, and these phrases can help.

Asking for Information

Is there a (travel service office) nearby?	Fùjìn yǒu (lǚxíng shè) ma?
Where is the (long-distance bus station)?	(Chángtú qìchē zhàn) zài nǎr?
I'm looking for a (CITS) representative.	Wǒ xiǎng zhǎo (Guó Lǚ) de rén.
Which direction is the (train station)?	Qù (huǒchē zhàn) wǎng nǎge fāng xiàng zǒu?
Where am I supposed to go?	Wǒ gāi wǎng nǎli zǒu?
Where's a ticket office?	Shòupiàochù zàinǎr?

Identification

This is my (passport).	Zhè shì wǒde (hùzhào).
I'm traveling with my (wife or husband).	Wǒ shì hé wǒ (àirén) yìqǐ lái de.
We're all together.	Wǒmen dōu shì yìqǐ lái de.
I've come to (sightsee).	Wǒ shì lái (guānguāng) de.
I am going to (Shanghai).	Wǒ yào qù (Shànghǎi).
I will stay there (eight) days.	Wǒ yào zài nàli dāi (bā tiān).

Booking a Ticket

I'd like to buy (two) ticket(s) to [Xi'an].	Wǒ yào mǎi (liǎng) zhāng qù [Xī'ān] de piào.
I'd like a (round-trip) ticket.	Wǒ yào mǎi yì zhāng (láihuí)piào.
I'd like to leave on the (9th) and return on the [17th].	Wǒ (jiǔ hào) líkāi, [shíqīhào]huílái.
How much is a (one-way) ticket to [Tianjin]?	Qù [Tiānjīn] de (dānchéng) piào duōshao qián?
Are there (soft-sleeper) tickets available?	Hái yǒu (ruǎnwò) piào ma?
Is it an express train?	Shì tèkuài huǒchē ma?
I'd want an upper/middle/lower berth.	Yào shàng/zhōng/xià pù.

附近有旅行社吗?

长途汽车站在哪儿?

我想找国旅的人。

去火车站往哪个方向走?

我该往哪里走?
售票处在哪儿?

这是我的护照。
我是和我爱人一起来的。

我们都是一起来的。
我是来观光的。
我要去上海。
我要在那里呆八天。

我要买两张去西安的票。

我要买一张来回票。

我九号离开,
十七号回来。
去天津的单程票多少钱?

还有软卧票吗?

是特快火车吗?
要上/中/下铺。

International Airlines

Many international airlines now land in either Shanghai or Beijing. When booking a flight, you may need to know the Chinese name for your chosen airline. Here are the names and codes of some airlines with service to China.

Air Canada AC	*Jiānádà Guójì Hángkōng Gōngsī* 加拿大国际航空公司
Air France AF	*Fǎguó Hángkōng Gōngsī* 法国航空公司
British Airways BA	*Yīngguó Hángkōng Gōngsī* 英国航空公司
Japan Airlines JL	*Rìběn Hángkōng Gōngsī* 日本航空公司
Lufthansa German Airlines LH	*Déguó Hànshā Hángkōng Gōngsī* 德国汉莎航空公司
Philippine Airlines PR	*Fēilǜbīn Hángkōng Gōngsī* 菲律宾航空公司
Singapore Airlines SQ	*Xīnjiāpō Hángkōng Gōngsī* 新加坡航空公司
Swissair SR	*Ruìshì Hángkōng Gōngsī* 瑞士航空公司
Thai Airways International TG	*Tàiguó Guójì Hángkōng Gōngsī* 泰国航空公司
United Airlines UA	*Měiguó Liánhé Hángkōng Gōngsī* 美国联合航空公司

Is there a discount for (children)?	*(Xiǎohái) piào piányì diǎn ma?*
How many stopovers are there enroute?	*Lùshàng yào tíng jǐ zhàn?*
When is the next (express train)?	*Xià cì (tèkuài) shì shénme shíjiān de?*
When is the next (ship) to [Wuhan]?	*Qù (Wǔhàn) de xià bān (chuán) shì shénme shíjiān de?*
Is there a (morning) train?	*Yǒu (zǎochén) de huǒchē ma?*
Is there an (evening) flight?	*Yǒu (wǎnshang) de hángbān ma?*
When is the last bus to (Chengde)?	*Qù (Chéngdé) de zuìhòu yí tàng qìchē shì shénme shíjiān?*
How long does it take by (train)?	*Zuò (huǒchē) yào duō jiǔ?*
What time should I arrive at the (airport)?	*Wǒ gāi shénme shíhou dào (jīchǎng)?*

Waiting to Board

Where should I go to (check in)?	*Wǒ yīnggāi dào nǎr qù (bàn shǒuxù)?*
When will flight no. (123) take off?	*(Yìbǎièrshísān) cì hángbān shénme shíhou qǐfēi?*
When will train no. (45) depart?	*(Sìshíwǔ) cì huǒchē shénme shíhou kāi?*
When will the bus to (Beidaihe) leave?	*Qù (Běidàihé) de qìchē shénme shíhou kāi?*
When will the train to (Luoyang) leave?	*Qù (Luòyáng) de huǒchē shénme shíhou kāi?*

小孩票便宜点吗?

路上要停几站?

下次特快是什么时间的?

去武汉的下班船是什么时间的?

有早晨的火车吗?

有晚上的航班吗?

去承德的最后一趟汽车是什么时间?

坐火车要多久?

我该什么时候到机场?

我应该到哪儿去办手续?

123次航班什么时候起飞?

45次火车什么时候开?

去北戴河的汽车什么时候开?

去洛阳的火车什么时候开?

What Kind of Plane Is This?

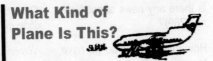

To meet the growing demands of visitors and business people who travel by air, the Civil Aviation Administration of China (CAAC) has been importing foreign aircraft as well as establishing joint ventures with foreign aircraft manufacturers. In the 1950s and 1960s, China's domestic routes were flown mainly by Soviet-made airplanes. Today, many of the planes are American or Western European models. You may ask the flight attendant, *Wǒmen zuò de fēijī shì shénme xínghào de?* (What kind of plane are we on?) and use the list below for reference.

Aerospace (British)	yǔháng gōngsī 宇航公司	
Airbus (European)	kōngzhōng kèchē 空中客车	
Antonov (Russia)	ān 安	
Boeing (USA)	bōyīn 波音	
Ilyushin (Russia)	yī'ěr 伊尔	
McDonnell Douglas (USA)	Màidào 麦道	
Shorts 360 (European)	xiāotè sānliùlíng 肖特三六〇	
Saab (Sweden)	sàbó 萨伯	

Is there any news about flight no. (789)?	(Qībǎi bāshí jiǔ) cì hángbān yǒu xiāoxi ma?
How much longer do we have to wait?	Wǒmen háiyào děng duōjiǔ?
Will I make the connecting flight?	Wǒ néng gǎnshàng xiánjiē hángbān ma?
Is there a (telephone) nearby?	Fùjìn yǒu (diànhuà) ma?
Please help me reroute my ticket.	Qǐng bāng wǒ gǎi yíxià hángbān.

All Aboard

Can you help me (store) this?	Nǐ néng bāng wǒ bǎ zhège (cún qǐlái) ma?
When will we arrive at (Lhasa)?	Wǒmen shénme shíhou néng dào (Lāsà)?
How is the weather in (Chengdu)?	(Chéngdū) de tiānqì zěnmeyàng?
This (seat belt) is broken.	Zhège (ānquándài) huài le.
Can you turn on the (air-conditioning)?	Qǐng bǎ (kōngtiáo) dǎkāi hǎo ma?
Where are we now?	Wǒmen xiànzài dào nǎli le?
What is that outside?	Wàimiàn nàge shì shénme?
What is the next station?	Xià zhàn shì nǎli?
What kind of (plane) is this?	Zhège (fēijī) shì shénme xínghào?
Will you please let me know when we're almost at (Suzhou)?	Kuài dào (Sūzhōu) de shíhòu qǐng tōngzhī wǒ yíxià.
How long will we stop here?	Wǒmen yào zài zhèli tíng duōjiǔ?

789次航班有消息吗?

我们还要等多久?

我能赶上衔接航班吗?

附近有电话吗?

请帮我改一下航班。

你能帮我把这个存起来吗?

我们什么时候能到拉萨?

成都的天气怎么样?

这个安全带坏了。

请把空调打开好吗?

我们现在到哪里了?

外面那个是什么?

下站是哪里?

这个飞机是什么型号?

快到苏州的时候请通知我一下。

我们要在这里停多久?

Tupolev (Russia)	*tú* 图
Yakovlev (Russia)	*yǎkè* 雅克
Xinzhou (PRC)	*xīnzhōu* 新舟

Good, Better, Best

Comparatives and superlatives in Chinese are formed by adding an extra word or two to the original modifier. The pattern is always the same. For example:

good	*hǎo*
better	*hǎo yìdiǎn (yìxiē)*
even better	*gèng hǎo*
very good	*fēicháng hǎo*
best	*zuìhǎo*
fast	*kuài*
faster	*kuài yìdiǎn (yìxiē)*
even faster	*gèng kuài*
very fast	*fēicháng kuài*
fastest	*zuìkuài*

The Chinese culture being a polite one, the first way of suggesting something more than the original is by adding *yìdiǎn*(a little) or *yìxiē* (some) after the modifier, thus implying something somewhat better but not a lot better. A stronger version of the comparative is formed by inserting *gèng*(even) before the modifier. The superlative is formed by inserting the word *zuì* (most).

The Best in Life

Traditionally Chinese have regarded luck, wealth, longevity, and happiness as the four blessings in life. You will find these four characters appearing on many

| What time do we have to be back on board? | Wǒmen jǐdiǎn bìxū huílai? |
| I'd like to upgrade my ticket. | Wǒ xiǎng bǔ zhāng (wòpù) piào. |

Baggage Claim

Where is the (baggage claim area)?	(Xíngli tíqǔ chu) zài nǎr?
I can't find my (suitcase).	Wǒde (xiāngzi) zhǎo bú dào le.
This is my (baggage claim tag).	Zhè shì wǒde (xíngli pái).
Are there any (carts)?	Yǒu (xiǎo tuīchē) ma?
Can someone help me (carry my bags)?	Yǒu rén néng bāng wǒ (tíyíxià xíngli) ma?
Where is the (exit)?	(Chūkǒu) zài nǎr?

Customs

This is mine.	Zhè shì wǒde.
This is not mine.	Zhè bú shì wǒde.
These are my (personal effects).	Zhè shì wǒde (sīrén wùpǐn).
I am not carrying any (precious jewelry).	Wǒ méi dài rènhé (zhūbǎo).
This is a (reproduction).	Zhè shì (fùzhìpǐn).
I'm not familiar with (these regulations).	Wǒ bú tài shúxī (zhèxiē guīdìng).
It's in my (wife's) suitcase.	Zài wǒ (qīzi de) xiāngzilǐ.
I lost it.	Diū le.
I gave it away.	Sòng rén le.
This is my (first) trip to China this year.	Zhè shì wǒ jīnnián (dì yī) cì lái Zhōngguó.
How much is the duty?	Shuìkuǎn duōshao?

我们几点必须回来?

我想补张(卧铺)票。

行李提取处在哪儿?

我的箱子找不到了。

这是我的行李牌。

有小推车吗?

有人能帮我提一下行李吗?

出口在哪儿?

这是我的。

这不是我的。

这是我的私人物品。

我没带任何珠宝。

这是复制品。

我不太熟悉这些规定。

在我妻子的箱子里。

丢了。

送人了。

这是我今年第一次来中国。

税款多少?

decorative objects, either singly or all four together.

福	fú	(luck)
禄	lù	(wealth)
寿	shòu	(longevity)
喜	xǐ	(happiness)

Good-byes

There are many ways to say good-bye in Chinese. Here are some of the most often used ones.

Huítóu jiàn.	See you soon.
Míngtiān jiàn.	See you tomorrow.
Xià cì jiàn.	See you next time.
Yíhuìr jiàn.	See you later.
Zàijiàn.	See you again.

What you'll Hear

Dào le.	We've arrived.
Gèwèi lǚkè qǐng zhùyì	Attention travelers...
Nǐ qù nǎr?	Where are you going?
Qǐng náchū nǐde...	Please show your...
dēngjī pái	boarding pass
hǎiguān shēnbàodān	customs declaration
hùzhào	passport
qiānzhèng	visa
zhàoxiàngjī	camera
Shì nǐde ma?	Is this yours?

17

Signs

jīchǎng
Airport

hòuchēshì
**Waiting Room
(for trains, buses)**

kāiwǎng...
Leaving for...

fēiyǐnyòng shuǐ
Unpotable Water

jìnzhǐ xīyān
No Smoking

3 Local Transport

In China, local transportation is available in many forms. You can get around town by taxi, hired car, public bus, bicycle, or "bus no. **11**," which simply means walking ("**11**" representing two legs). In Beijing, Shanghai, and Guangzhou you can also ride the subway, or dìtiě. The most important thing to learn is how to ask for directions, and then understanding the answer.

Getting Set

I'd like a (local) map, please.	*Qǐng gěi wǒ yì zhāng (běndì) dìtú.*
Can I get some directions?	*Néng wèn yíxià lù ma?*
I'd like to go to (the Big Goose Pagoda).	*Wǒ xiǎng qù (Dàyàn Tǎ).*
What's the best way to get there?	*Něi tiáo lù zuìjìn?*
How far is it to (People's Park)?	*Qù (Rénmín Gōngyuán) yǒu duōyuǎn?*
Is it within walking distance?	*Zǒu de dào ma?*
How much should the fare be to (the airport)?	*Qù (jīchǎng) yào duōshǎo qián?*
Please show me where we are on this map.	*Qǐng gàosù wǒ wǒmen zài dìtú shàng de nǎr?*

Taking a Taxi

Where can I get a taxi?	*Nǎr néng jiàodào chūzūchē?*
Can you send a taxi?	*Nǐmen néngpài liàng chūzūchē ma?*
I'd like a cab to (the Exhibition Center).	*Wǒ yàoqù (zhǎnlǎn zhōngxīn).*
What's the fare per kilometer?	*Yì gōnglǐ duōshao qián?*
To (the Peace Hotel), please.	*Qǐng kāi dào (Hépíng Fàndiàn).*
Driver, can you take me to (this address)?	*Sījī, nǐ néng bǎ wǒ sòng dào (zhège dìfāng) ma?*
Do you know the way there?	*Nǐ zhīdao zěnme zǒu ma?*
Please stop a moment.	*Qǐng tíng yíxià.*
Please drive (faster).	*Qǐng kāi (kuài yìdiǎn).*
Make a right at the light.	*Zài hónglùdēng yòu zhuǎn.*
(Please) slow down.	*(Qǐng kāi) màn yídiǎn.*
Wait!	*Děng yìhuǐr!*
Stop!	*Tíng!*
Does luggage cost extra?	*Xínglǐ lìngwài shōufèi ma?*

请给我一张本地地图。

能问一下路吗？

我想去大雁塔。

哪条路最近？

去人民公园有多远？

走得到吗？

去机场要多少钱？

请告诉我我们在地图上的哪儿？

哪儿能叫到出租车？

你们能派辆出租车吗？

我要去展览中心。

一公里多少钱？

请开到和平饭店。

司机，你能把我送到这个地方吗？

你知道怎么走吗？

请停一下。

请开快一点。

在红绿灯右转。

(请开)慢点。

等一会儿。

停！

行李另外收费吗？

Which Way Is North?

After you ask someone on the street for directions, listen for these key words in their answer:

北	běi	north
东	dōng	east
南	nán	south
西	xī	west
右	yòu	right
左	zuǒ	left
后	hòu	back
前	qián	front

Some common expressions used for giving directions are:

guò…	past (across)...
hóng lù dēng	the stoplight
mǎ lù	the road
wǎng… guǎi	turn toward...
wǎng… zǒu	walk toward...
yìzhí zǒu	go straight on
zài… biān	on the ... side
zài… miàn	facing the...
zǒu cuò le	wrong way

Taxi Fares

In China, every legitimate taxi is metered. Most taxis belong to state-owned taxi companies, which operate either as independent car services or in connection with travel agencies, hotels, or restaurants. Recently there has been a rise of gypsy cabs on the streets, be careful of them. When you enter a cab, make sure the driver turns on the meter. If he doesn't, say *Qǐng dǎkāi jìjiàqì* (please turn on the meter). If he still refuses to turn on the meter, the best you can do is strike a hard bargain for the fare to your destination, or get out of the cab.

Can you wait for me?	*Néng děng wǒ yíxià ma?*
I'll be back in (20) minutes.	*Wǒ (èrshí) fēnzhōng yǐhòu huílai.*
Then I'd like to return to (the hotel).	*Ránhòu wǒ jiù huí (fàndiàn).*
This is the wrong way.	*Zǒu cuò lù le.*
Don't try to trick me.	*Bié piàn wǒ.*

Hiring a Car

I'd like to hire (a car).	*Wǒ yào bāo (yí liàng chē).*
What is the rate per (day)?	*Měi (tiān) duōshao zūjīn?*
Can I hire a car for (half a day)?	*Bāo (bàntiān) chē xíng ma?*
I'd like to rent a car one way.	*Wǒ xiǎng zū dānchéng chē.*
After how many (kilometers) will there be an extra charge?	*Chāoguò duōshao (gōnglǐ) yào lìngwài jiā qián?*
How do you charge for extra (mileage)?	*Chāoguò de (lǐchéng) zěnme shōufèi?*
Do you have a car available (now)?	*(Xiànzài) yǒu chē ma?*
I'd like to hire a car for (two) days beginning [the day after tomorrow].	*Wǒ xiǎng cóng [hòutiān] qǐ bāo (liǎng) tiān chē.*
I'll come for the car at (8:00 in the morning).	*(Zǎochén bā diǎn) wǒ yào yòng chē.*
Buckle up!	*Qǐng jì shàng ānquán dài.*
Fill'er up!	*Jiā mǎn yóu!*
I have a flat tire.	*Wǒ de lúntāi méi qì le.*
My car broke down on the freeway.	*Wǒ de chē zài gāosù gōnglù shàng pāo máo le.*

能等我一下吗?

我二十分钟以后回来。

然后我就回饭店。

走错路了。

别骗我。

我要包一辆车。

每天多少租金?

包半天车行吗?

我想租单程车。

超过多少公里要另外加钱?

超过的里程怎么收费?

现在有车吗?

我想从后天起包两天车。

早晨八点我要用车。

请系上安全带。

加满油!

我的轮胎没气了。

我的车在高速公路上抛锚了。

Two decades ago, taxis were rare in Beijing, but nowadays you can see yellow or red cabs filling the street. They are reasonable and convenient. There are several types of taxis in the street, including Elantra, Sonata, Hongqi (Red Flag) and Elysee, all charging 2 yuan per kilometer.

Bus Numbers

Buses in China are identified by their route number, so instead of saying *hào* (number) when referring to a bus, the Chinese say *lù* (route). Thus, bus no. 52 would be *wǔshíèr lù chē*.

Riding Public Buses

Public buses are the chief means of local transportation for Chinese urban residents. Downtown buses and trolleys (1-126) have a flat rate fare of 1 yuan and run between approximately 5am and 11pm; night services (201-212) have a flat rate fare of 1 yuan and run between 11pm and 4:30am. For most other routes, prices start from 1 yuan and depend on the distance traveled. The first bus is usually between 5 am and 6 am and the last comes around 8pm to 11pm. After boarding a bus, tell the conductor how many tickets you want and to what destination; for example, *Liǎng zhāng, Tiān ān mén* (two tickets, Tian'anmen). He or she will tell you the price, such as 2 yuan, and give you a ticket stub. Keep the stub in case you need to show it later.

A public transport Superpass (yikatong) may help save your money and time buying individual tickets. You can buy a superpass at China Post offices, subway

Going by Bus

Which bus should I take to get to (the Summer Palace)?	*Qù (Yíhéyuán) zuò něi lù chē?*
Where is the nearest bus stop?	*Zuìjìn de gōnggòng qìchē zhàn zài nǎr?*
How many stops to (the zoo)?	*Qù (Dòngwùyuán) yǒu jǐ zhàn?*
Does this bus go to the (National Library)?	*Zhè tàng chē qù (Guojia Túshūguǎn) ma?*
(One) ticket.	*(Yì) zhāng.*
Please tell me to get off when it gets to (Wangfujing).	*Dào (Wángfǔjǐng) zhàn qǐng jiào wǒ yíxià.*
Where can I transfer to bus no. (302)?	*Zài nǎr néng dǎo (sān líng èr) lù chē?*
Where is the bus stop for bus no. (41)?	*(Sìshí yī) lù chēzhàn zài nǎr?*
I came by the city streets.	*Wǒ shì zǒu shìqū dàolù lái de.*
I was tied up in traffic.	*Wǒ yù dào sāi chē.*

Riding the Subway

Is this a subway (entrance)?	*Zhè shì dìtiě de (rùkǒu) ma?*
Does this subway go to (Chongwenmen)?	*Zhè tàng ditiě qù (Chóngwénmén) ma?*
Where should I wait for the subway to (Beijing Railway Station)?	*Qù (Běijīng Zhàn) zài nǎr děng chē?*
What is the next stop?	*Xià zhàn shì nǎr?*
Make way please, we want to get off.	*Qǐng ràng yíxià, wǒmen yào xià chē.*

去颐和园坐哪路车？

最近的公共汽车站在哪儿？

去动物园有几站？

这趟车去国家图书馆吗？

一张。

到王府井站请叫我一下。

在哪儿能倒302路车？

41路车站在哪儿？

我是走市区道路来的。

我遇到塞车。

这是地铁的入口吗？

这趟地铁去崇文门吗？

去北京站在哪儿等车？

下站是哪儿？

请让一下，我们要下车。

stations or CITIC Bank branches. There is a refundable 20 yuan deposit per card. Three types of pre-paid superpasses are now available:

Adults card for buses numbered from 1 to 899, 40% of the normal ticket prices. Subways, no discount. No limit on duration.

Students card for buses numbered from 1 to 899, 20% of the normal ticket prices. Subways, no discount. No Limit on duration.

Limited duration bus cards are very handy for visitors: a 3-day card (maximum 18 rides) costs 10 yuan; a 7-day card (maximum 42 rides) costs 20 yuan; and a 15-day card (maximum 90 rides) costs 40 yuan.

When you have almost reached your stop, be sure to make your way to the door. On crowded buses it's easy to get packed in the middle of the bus and not be able to get off before the doors close and the bus moves on.

Bus Stops

Bus stops are marked by signposts at bus shelters along the road. If the road is wide and an island separates it from the bicycle path, the bus stop will be on the island. The bus sign will show the route number, the times of the first run and last run, the name of the current stop, and all the stops along the route. The direction toward which the bus is traveling is indicated by an arrow.

Some Chinese characters you will need to recognize are:

公共汽车	public bus
本站	this stop
下站	next stop
头班车	first run
首班车	first run
末班车	last run
夜班车	night bus

On Foot

I'm trying to find (Elephant Trunk Hill).	*Wǒ zài zhǎo (Xiàngbí shān).*
Can you direct me there?	*Nǐ néng gàosù wǒ zěnme zǒu ma?*
Does this lane lead to (the main street)?	*Zhètiáo xiǎoxiàng tōngxiàng (dàjiē) ma?*
Excuse me, could you tell me where the (CAAC office) is?	*Láojià nǐ néng gàosù wǒ (Zhōngguó Mínháng bànshìchù) zài nǎr ma?*
Is this (Chang'an Avenue)?	*Zhè shì (Cháng'ān Jiē) ma?*
Is this way (north)?	*Zhè shì (běi) miàn ma?*
I'm lost.	*Wǒ mílù le.*
Where am I?	*Wǒ xiànzài zài nǎr?*

Renting a Bike

It used to be easy to rent a bike, but these days, few places rent bikes.

I'd like to rent a bicycle.	*Wǒ xiǎng zū yī liàng zìxíngchē.*
How much is the rental for one (hour)?	*Yì (xiǎo shí) de zūjīn shì duōshao?*
How much is (the deposit)?	*(Yājīn) duōshao?*
I'd like that (blue) one.	*Wǒ yào nà liàng (lán) de.*
I'll bring it back around (4:00 in the afternoon).	*(Xiàwǔ sì diǎn) zuǒyòu wǒ lái huán chē.*
I've finished riding.	*Wǒ bú yòng chē le.*
How much do I owe?	*Duōshao qián?*
My (passport), please.	*Qǐng bǎ (hùzhào) huán wǒ.*
Where can I rent a bicycle?	*Zài nǎr néng zū zìxíngchē?*
(I've got) a flat tire.	*Lúntāi biě le.*

26

Bicycle

The bicycle is the most popular means of transport in China. Nearly everybody has one. A great mass of people in city go to work by bike. It is a feast for eyes if you get up early in the morning and watch the great masses of bicycle streaming down the street. You may be able to hire a bike at your hotel and riding around the streets is great fun, especially if you are going to visit the hutongs. But you have to be careful, especially at junctions and traffic lights. Traffic in China is sometimes chaotic and rules about right of way and turning right at traffic lights may be different from your own country, so it is potentially confusing and dangerous, so take care.

我在找象鼻山。

你能告诉我怎么走吗？

这条小巷通向大街吗？

劳驾，你能告诉我中国民航办事处在哪儿吗？

这是长安街吗？

这是北面吗？

我迷路了。

我现在在哪儿？

我想租一辆自行车。

一小时的租金是多少？

押金多少？

我要那辆蓝的。

下午四点左右我来还车。

我不用车了。

多少钱？

请把护照还我。

在哪儿能租自行车？

轮胎瘪了。

What You'll Hear

chūshì piào	show your ticket
dǎo chē	transfer buses
Dào nǎr?	Where to?
huàn chē	transfer buses
Kàn chē!	Watch out (for the bike or car)!
kuài chē	express
mǎi piào	buy a ticket
Xià ma?	Are you getting off?
Xiān xià, hòu shàng.	Let people off first, then get on.
Zhàn zhù.	Halt.

Signs

chūzūqìchē zhàn
Taxi Stand

zìxíngchē xiūlǐbù
Bicycle Repair Shop

tíng
No Parking

chū rù qing xià chē
Please Get off Your Bike at the Gate

shìgù duōfā dìduàn
Site of Frequent Accidents

4 Hotel

Hotels have come a long way in China, especially since the early 1980s when Western tourists began arriving in big waves. Whereas a "first-class hotel" used to mean a 1950s-style boardinghouse with simple furniture, clean bedding, and keys hung on a pegboard, these days it means a five-star hotel where you can find everything from broadband Internet access to health and sports clubs and conference rooms. The service people at the main desk usually know enough English to handle common requests.

Checking In

I have already booked (one) room for [two] nights.	*Wǒ yǐjīng yùdìng le (yí) gè fángjiān zhù liǎng gè wǎnshang.*
Do you have a (single room) available?	*Yǒu (dān jiān) ma?*
How much is a (twin room) per night?	*(Shuāngrén fángjiān) duōshao qián?*
What is your lowest rate for a room?	*(Zuìpiányi) de fángjiān shì duō shao qián?*
I would like to stay (three) nights.	*Wǒ xiǎng zhù (sān) tiān.*
I would like (two) rooms next to each other.	*Wǒ yào (liǎng) gè jǐnāizhe de fángjiān.*
I would like a room facing the (garden).	*Wǒ yào yì jiān chuānghu duìzhe (huāyuán) de fángjiān.*
Does this room have a good (view)?	*Zhège fángjiān (chuāngwài de fēngjǐng) hǎo ma?*
I prefer a room on a (lower) floor.	*Wǒ xiǎng yào (dī) céng de fángjiān.*
Can an extra cot be brought in?	*Néng zàijiā yì zhāng chuáng ma?*
Do you give a discount to (foreign students)?	*Duì (liúxuéshēng) yǒu méi yǒu yōuhuì?*
Will I be able to pay by (credit card)?	*Wǒ néng yòng (xìnyòngkǎ) fùkuǎn ma?*

Checking Out

Please make up my bill.	*Qǐng bāng wǒ jiézhàng.*
My room number is (3024).	*Wǒ zhù (sān líng èr sì) fángjiān.*

我已经预定了一个房间，住两个晚上。

有单间吗？

双人房间多少钱？

最便宜的房间是多少钱？

我想住三天。

我要两个紧挨着的房间。

我要一间窗户对着花园的房间。

这个房间窗外的风景好吗？

我想要低层的房间。

能再加一张床吗？

对留学生有没有优惠？

我能用信用卡付款吗？

请帮我结帐。

我住3024房间。

Local Hostels

For those of you who are traveling on a shoestring you might choose to stay at a *zhāodàisuǒ* (hostel), *lǚguǎn* (small hotel), *lǚshè* (inn), or *sùshè* (dorm or hostel). The prices there are cheap, the most you'll pay being 60 yuan for a single room to 20 yuan for a room shared with three other people. The accommodations are Spartan with a bathroom down the hallway. Remember also that running hot water is a luxury in many places in China, so some small establishments will not have it. When hot water is provided, the hours are usually restricted.

To request a bed in a shared room, use the phrase *Hái yǒu chuáng wèi ma?* (Is there a berth available?)

Chinese Zodiac

The Chinese zodiac is represented by twelve animals, with one animal governing each year in a twelve-year cycle. Each animal represents one of the Twelve Earthly Branches in Chinese astrology.

Traditionally, Chinese have kept track of each other's ages by remembering what animal sign a person belongs to. For example, someone might forget how old his sister is but remember "Oh, she was born in the year of the tiger..." and figure it out from there. If you want to ask someone's age indirectly, say *Nǐ shǔ shén mè?* (what do you belong to?) The twelve animals and their corresponding years in the 20th century and early 21st century are listed below.

There seems to be a mistake here.	*Zhèli hǎoxiàng yǒu diǎn bú duì.*
I've paid already.	*Wǒ yǐjīng fù guò kuǎn le.*
When is check-out time?	*Shénme shíhou tuì fáng?*
I'll be leaving tomorrow morning at (7:30).	*Wǒ míngtiān zǎochén (qī diǎnbàn) zǒu.*
Where shall I leave the key?	*Yàoshi liú zài nǎr?*
Put it on my hotel bill, please.	*Qǐng suànzài wǒde zhùsùfèi li.*

Service Inquiries

When will my (suitcases) be brought up?	*Wǒde (xíngli)shénme shíhou néng sòng shàng lái?*
Can it be brought to my room?	*Néng sòngdào wǒde fángjiān ma?*
Where shall I pick up (the keys)?	*Wǒ dào nǎr qù ná (yàoshi)?*
Do you have another (key) for my roommate?	*Néng gěi wǒde tóngwū (yì bǎ yàoshi) ma?*
Have there been any messages for me?	*Yǒu rén gěi wǒ liúhuà ma?*
Where is the (elevator)?	*(Diàntī) zài nǎr?*
When is the (bar) open?	*(Jiǔbā) shénme shíhou kāimén?*
Do you have today's (China Daily)?	*Yǒu jīntiān de (Zhōngguó Rìbào) ma?*
Where can I find (the banquet manager)?	*Nǎr néng zhǎo dào (yànhuìtīng jīnglǐ)?*
Is there some place where I can send (email)?	*Nǎr néng fā (diànzǐ yóujiàn)?*
Can you help me get my (watch) repaired?	*Nǐ néng bāng wǒ xiū yíxià (biǎo) ma?*

这里好像有点不对。

我已经付过款了。

什么时候退房?

我明天早晨七点半走。

钥匙留在哪儿?

请算在我的住宿费里。

我的行李什么时候能送上来?

能送到我的房间吗?

我到哪儿去拿钥匙?

能给我的同屋一把钥匙吗?

有人给我留话吗?

电梯在哪儿?

酒吧什么时候开门?

有今天的《中国日报》吗?

哪儿能找到宴会厅经理?

哪儿能发电子邮件?

你能帮我修一下表吗?

Rat	鼠	1900, 1912, 1924, 1936, 1948
shǔ		1960, 1972, 1984, 1996, 2008
Ox	牛	1901, 1913, 1925, 1937, 1949
niú		1961, 1973, 1985, 1997, 2009
Tiger	虎	1902, 1914, 1926, 1938, 1950
hǔ		1962, 1974, 1986, 1998, 2010
Rabbit	兔	1903, 1915, 1927, 1939, 1951
tù		1963, 1975, 1987, 1999, 2011
Dragon	龙	1904, 1916, 1928, 1940, 1952
lóng		1964, 1976, 1988, 2000, 2012
Snake	蛇	1905, 1917, 1929, 1941, 1953
shé		1965, 1977, 1989, 2001, 2013
Horse	马	1906, 1918, 1930, 1942, 1954
mǎ		1966, 1978, 1990, 2002, 2014
Sheep	羊	1907, 1919, 1931, 1943, 1955
yáng		1967, 1979, 1991, 2003, 2015
Monkey	猴	1908, 1920, 1932, 1944, 1956
hóu		1968, 1980, 1992, 2004, 2016
Rooster	鸡	1909, 1921, 1933, 1945, 1957
jī		1969, 1981, 1993, 2005, 2017
Dog	狗	1910, 1922, 1934, 1946, 1958
gǒu		1970, 1982, 1994, 2006, 2018
Pig	猪	1911, 1923, 1935, 1947, 1959
zhū		1971, 1983, 1995, 2007, 2019

Long-distance Communications

Post offices in China are the centers for long-distance telephone calls and telegrams. If you are far away from a luxury hotel and need to call home, go to a main post office. However, be prepared to wait in line to place your call or telegram. International phone calls sometimes take some time for the connection to be made.

Please wake me up tomorrow at (6:00).	*Qǐng zài míngtiān zǎochén (liù diǎn) jiào xǐng wǒ.*

Problems in the Room

The (toilet) doesn't work.	*(Mǎtǒng) huài le.*
The (faucet) is leaking.	*(Lóngtóu) lòushuǐ.*
Please help me open the (windows).	*Qǐng bāng wǒ dǎkāi (chuānghu).*
The door doesn't lock.	*Zhèige mén suǒ bú shàng.*
How do you turn on the (heat)?	*Zěnme kāi (nuǎnqì)?*
How do you adjust this (digital clock)?	*Zhège (diànzǐbiǎo) zěnme tiáo?*
My room is too (noisy).	*Wǒde fángjiān tài (chǎo) le.*
I'd like to change to another room.	*Wǒ xiǎng huàn yí gè fángjiān.*

Housekeeping

I need (some towels).	*Wǒ xiǎng yào (jǐ tiáo máojīn).*
May I borrow an (iron)?	*Wǒ xiǎngjiè yí gè (yùndǒu).*
Please bring (a thermos of boiled water).	*Qǐng ná (yì píng kāishuǐ) lái.*
May I have another (blanket)?	*Néng zài gěi wǒ (yì tiáo tǎnzi) ma?*
The room needs to be cleaned.	*Zhège fángjiān gāi dǎsǎo le.*
Could you vacuum the (rug)?	*Qǐng bǎ (dìtǎn) xī yíxià.*
Please take this away.	*Qǐng bǎ zhèige ná zǒu.*
This plug doesn't fit.	*Zhèige chātóu chā bú shàng.*
What shall I do?	*Zěnme bàn?*

请在明天早晨六点叫醒我。

马桶坏了。

龙头漏水。

请帮我打开窗户。

这个门锁不上。

怎么开暖气?

这个电子表怎么调?

我的房间太吵了。

我想换一个房间。

我想要几条毛巾。

我想借一个熨斗。

请拿一瓶开水来。

能再给我一条毯子吗?

这个房间该打扫了。

请把地毯吸一下。

请把这个拿走。

这个插头插不上。

怎么办?

English-language Publications

Several English-language magazines and newspapers are published in China. There are also expat magazines in many major cities. Many hotels offer a selection of these publications free of charge. The well-known ones are:

China Daily

Established in 1981, this is the only national English-language newspaper in China and is regarded as one of the country's most authoritative English media outlets and an important source of information on Chinese politics, economy, society and culture.

Beijing Review

Established in 1958, this is China's only English weekly news magazine. The magazine is available in a printed edition in English and online editions in Chinese, English, French, German and Japanese.

China Pictorial

Founded in 1950, this highly illustrated magazine focuses on tourism, culture and social life. It produces printed and online editions in English, Chinese and other languages.

China Today

Originally titled *China Reconstructs* and founded in 1952 by Soong Ching Ling (Mme. Sun Yat-sen) to promote understanding and friendship between the Chinese people and the rest of the world, this comprehensive monthly reports on the lives of everyday people and the social development of China.

Laundry

This is my laundry.	Zhè shì wǒ yào xǐ de yīfu.
When will I get my laundry back?	Yīfu shénme shíhou néng xǐ hǎo?
Can it be done sooner?	Néng kuài yìdiǎn ma?
I need it (tonight).	Wǒ (jīntiān wǎnshang) yào.
This is to be (dry cleaned).	Zhèi jiàn yào (gānxǐ).
This should be (hand washed).	Zhèi jiàn yào (shǒuxǐ).

Making a Phone Call

Hello!	Wèi!
Who's calling?	Nǐ shi shui?
It's...	Wǒ shi ...
He/She's (not) here.	Tā (bú) zài.
I'll call back later.	Wǒ yǐhòu zàidǎ.
Hello, do you speak English?	Wèi, nǐ huì shuō yīngwén ma?
Hello, is (Li) there?	Wèi, Lǐ zàima?
Yes, hang on a minute.	Tā zài, qǐng děng yī huìr.
How much longer will I have to wait?	Hái yào děng duōjiǔ?
Your call didn't go through.	Nǐ de diànhuà méiyǒu jiētōng.

这是我要洗的衣服。

衣服什么时候能洗好?

能快一点吗?

我今天晚上要。

这件要干洗。

这件要手洗。

喂!

你是谁?

我是……

他/她不在。

我以后再打。

喂,你会说英文吗?

喂,李在吗?

他在,请等一会儿。

还要等多久?

你的电话没有接通。

China Internet Information Center
http://www.china.org.cn
The authorized government portal site
to China, www.china.org.cn offers broad
access to up-to-date news about China,
with searchable texts of government
position papers and a wealth of basic information about Chinese history, politics,
economy and culture.

Chinese-language Newspapers

What do the Chinese read very day?
There are over one thousand registered
daily papers in China, published by various organizations at the national, provin-
cial, municipal, and autonomous regional
levels. The leading national newspapers
are:

人民日报
Rénmín Rìbào
(People's Daily)
This is the official newspaper of the CPC
Central Committee. It began publication
in 1947 in the North China Liberated
Area.

光明日报
GuāngMíng Rìbào
(Enlightenment Daily)
A newspaper mainly read by intellectuals,
it began publication in 1949 as the organ
of the All-China Democratic League and
in 1952 became the combined organ of
all the democratic parties.

Please cancel the call I booked.	*Qǐng qǔxiāo gāngcái wǒ yào de diànhuà.*
Please give me extension (800).	*Qǐng jiē (bā líng líng) fēnjī.*
Please connect me with (the main desk).	*Qǐng jiē (zǒng fúwùtái).*
The line is not clear.	*Diànhuà tīng bù qīngchǔ.*
It was a wrong number.	*Hàomǎ cuò le.*
My phone is out of order.	*Wǒde diànhuà chū gùzhàng le.*
Could you help me make a call?	*Nǐ néng bāng wǒ dǎ yí gè diànhuà ma?*
Do I need to dial "0" first?	*Yào xiān bō líng ma?*
Please connect me with the room of Mr. Brown.	*Qǐng bǎ diànhuà zhuǎn dào Brown xiānshēng de fángjiān.*

The Foreign Exchange Desk

I'd like to convert (US dollars).	*Wǒ yào duìhuàn (Měiyuán).*
I have (traveler's checks).	*Wǒ yǒu (lǚxíng zhīpiào).*
Do you accept (credit cards)?	*Néng yòng (xìnyòngkǎ) ma?*
Please give me (large) bills.	*Qǐng gěi wǒ (dà) piàozi.*
Please give me (20 yuan) in small bills and change.	*Qǐng gěi wǒ (èrshí yuán) líng qián.*
May I have (a receipt)?	*Néng gěi wǒ (yì zhāng fāpiào) ma?*
Where can I get a cash advance on my credit card?	*Nǎr néng yòng xìnyòngkǎ duìhuàn xiànjīn?*

请取消刚才我要的
电话。

请接800分机。

请接总服务台。

电话听不清楚。

号码错了。

我的电话出故障了。

你能帮我打一个电话吗？

要先拨"0"吗？

请把电话转到Brown
先生的房间。

我要兑换美元。

我有旅行支票。

能用信用卡吗？

请给我大票子。

请给我二十元零钱。

能给我一张发票吗？

哪儿能用信用卡兑换现
金？

经济日报
Jīngjì Rìbào
(Economic Daily)
Founded in 1983, this newspaper reports on China's economic developments, reforms, products, and markets.

参考消息
Cānkǎo Xiāoxi
(News Reference)
Widely read by people of all ages, this bulletin reports new developments in international politics and economy, with translations of articles from foreign presses. It originated as a pamphlet published in Yan'an in the 1930s.

中国体育报
Zhongguo Tǐyù Bào
(China Sports Daily)
Founded in 1958, this is China's only nationwide sports newspaper. It is published by China Sports Newspapers Group directly affiliated to the State Physical Culture Administration.

Post Office Tips

Here are some helpful hints for mailing letters in China:

● Envelopes are not pre-glued on the back flap, so be sure to seal your letters by using the glue provided at the post office or in your room. Licking the back of the envelope will not work.

● The smaller denominations of postage stamps, used on domestic mail, do not have glue on the back. Again, use the glue pot.

● When you mail a letter overseas, make sure the country of destination is clearly written; if possible, include the Chinese characters for that country.

Where can I cash a (personal check)?	Zài nǎr néng duìhuàn (zhīpiào)?
Is this a (service fee)?	Zhè shì (fúwù fèi) ma?
What is the exchange rate?	Duìhuàn lǜ shì duōshao?

The Post Office

I'd like to mail (a letter).	Wǒ yào jì (xìn).
I'd like to buy (five) [80 fen] stamps.	Wǒ yào mǎi (wǔ) zhāng bā máo de yóupiào.
Please give me (three) [1.60 yuan] stamps.	Qǐng mài gěi wǒ (sān) zhāng [yí kuài liù] de yóupiào.
How much does it cost to mail a (postcard)?	Jì míngxìnpiàn yào duōshao qián?
Please send it (air mail).	Wǒ jì (hángkōng) xìn.
I want this letter sent by express.	Zhè fēng xìn wǒ yào jì tèkuàizhuāndì.
How long will it take this (package) to arrive?	Zhè (bāoguǒ) duōjiǔ néngdào?
Can you write the (name of the country) in Chinese for me?	Qǐng bāng wǒ bǎ (guómíng) xiě chéng Zhōngwén.
Can you help me wrap this?	Nǐ néng bāng wǒ bāo yíxià ma?
Do you have some (string)?	Yǒu (shéngzi) ma?
I would like to buy some (commemorative stamps).	Wǒ xiǎng mǎi yìxiē (jìniàn yóupiào).
Do you have (the whole set)?	Yǒu (quán tào de) ma?
When is the mail collected?	Yóudìyuán shénme shíjiān lái qǔ xìn?
Please send this parcel registered.	Qǐng yòng guàhào jì zhèige bāoguǒ.

在哪儿能兑换支票？

这是服务费吗？

兑换率是多少？

我要寄信。

我要买五张八毛的邮票。

请卖给我三张一块六的邮票。

寄明信片要多少钱？

我寄航空信。

这封信我要寄特快专递。

这包裹多久能到？

请帮我把国名写成中文。

你能帮我包一下吗？

有绳子吗？

我想买一些纪念邮票。

有全套的吗？

邮递员什么时间来取信？

请用挂号寄这个包裹。

Tea

The most popular beverage in China is tea. Tea is said to have many curative effects, from improving eyesight and preventing tooth decay to helping reduce weight. Below are the names of the basic teas in China.

lǜchá 绿茶
Green Tea: an unfermented tea with a clear taste and dark green color. The most famous green tea is West Lake Dragon Well Tea (*xīhú lóngjǐngchá*) produced in Hangzhou. It is known for its delicate taste.

hóngchá 红茶
Black Tea: a fermented tea with a fruit fragrance and mellow taste. A famous black tea is Keemun Tea (*qíhóng*) produced in Qimen, Anhui Province. It has a sweet aftertaste.

wūlóngchá 乌龙茶
Oolong Tea: a semi-fermented tea produced in Fujian and Taiwan. A famous oolong tea is Iron Goddess of Mercy Tea (*tiěguānyīnchá*) which has a sweet aroma and concentrated taste.

huāchá 花茶
Scented Tea: a tea produced by smoke-processing tea leaves with flower petals. Jasmine Tea (*mòlìhuāchá*) is popular for its clear taste and jasmine fragrance.

zhuānchá 砖茶
Brick Tea: tea that is pressed into the shape of a brick, or other shape, after the tea leaves have been steamed. Easy to carry and store, this tea has a strong taste and can dissolve fat. It is an indispensable beverage for national minorities that eat a lot of meat.

Faxes

Do you have a (fax machine)?   *Yǒu (chuánzhēnjī) ma?*

May I send it myself?   *Wǒ kěyǐ zìjǐ fā ma?*

I don't know how to use a (fax machine).   *Wǒ bù huì yòng (chuánzhēnjī).*

The Barbershop

I need a (haircut).   *Wǒ yào (lǐfà).*

Please give me a (trim).   *Qǐng bāng wǒ (xiūjiǎn) yíxià.*

I'd like it rather (short).   *Wǒ yào (duǎn) diǎn.*

Please cut more (here).   *(Zhè biān) duō jiǎn diǎn.*

Please leave it long (here).   *(Zhè biān) yào cháng diǎn.*

Please do not use (conditioner).   *Qǐng bú yào yòng (hùfàsù).*

Please (blow dry) my hair.   *Qǐng bǎ tóufà (chuīgān).*

I'd like to have a (New Wave) look.   *Wǒ xiǎng yào (xīncháo) fàshì.*

有传真机吗？

我可以自己发吗？

我不会用传真机。

我要理发。

请帮我修剪一下。

我要短点。

这边多剪点。

这边要长点。

请不要用护发素。

请把头发吹干。

我想要新潮发式。

Batteries

Ran out of batteries? Don't worry, the common sizes of batteries are available in most local department stores.
However, in China they are named not by alphabet but by number. Here's how to request the battery you want:

D battery (# 1)	*yī hào diànchí*
C battery (# 2)	*èr hào diànchí*
AA battery (# 5)	*wǔ hào diànchí*
AAA battery (# 7)	*qī hào diànchí*

What You'll Hear

diànhuà fèi	telephone bill
fúwùtái	service desk
fúwùyuán	service attendant
Jǐ lóu?	Which floor?
lóushàng	upstairs
lóuxià	downstairs
Méi rén jiē.	No answer. (phone)
Xiān bō líng.	Dial "0" first.
zhàn xiàn	busy line (phone)

43

Signs

饭店
fàndiàn
Hotel

开门
kāi mén
Open

关门
guān mén
Closed

拉
lā
Pull

推 推
tuī
Push

五 wǔ **5** Friends

> **Chī le ma?**
> How's it going? (Eaten yet?)

In most places, you will get a warm and friendly response to your enthusiasm trying speaking Chinese. A conversation can be struck and new acquaintances made with just a few simple words.

The most often used greeting, appropriate for all occasions, is nǐ hǎo (hello). Around mealtimes, Chinese often greet each other with Chī le ma? (Have you eaten yet?) which is a general expression of concern for the other person. The proper reply, even if you haven't eaten for days, is Chī le, xièxie (I've eaten, thanks).

Opening Lines

Hello!	*Nǐhǎo!*
How are you?	*Nǐ hǎo ma?*
(Fine), and you?	*Hěn hǎo, nǐ ne?*
So-so.	*Hái kěyǐ.*
Not too bad.	*Bú cuò.*
Good morning.	*Zǎoshàng hǎo.*
Good evening.	*Wǎnshàng hǎo.*
Good night.	*Wǎn'ān.*
How old are you? (to a child)	*Nǐ jǐ suì?*
How old are you? (adult)	*Nǐ jīnnián duōdà?*
I'm (twenty-five) years old.	*Wǒ èrshíwǔ suì.*
Where are you from?	*Nǐ shì nǎli rén?*
I'm from (England).	*Wǒ shì Yīngguó rén.*
What do you think of (Australia)?	*Nǐ duì(Àodàlìyà)de yìnxiàng rúhé?*
This is my first trip to (China).	*Wǒ shì dìyī cì lái (Zhōngguó).*
I would like to learn some (Chinese).	*Wǒ xiǎng xué yìxiē (Zhōngwén).*

Talk About the Weather

It's a (fine) day today.	*Jīntiān tiānqì (tǐng hǎo).*
Wow, it's really pouring!	*Āiyā, yǔ xià de zhēn dà!*
Do you know what the weather forecast for (tomorrow) is?	*Nǐ zhīdao (míngtiān) de tiānqì yùbào ma?*
The weather report says it will be (cold).	*Tiānqì yùbào shuō míngtiān huì (lěng).*
Tomorrow it might (rain).	*Míngtiān kěnéng (xià yǔ).*

你好!

你好吗?

很好，你呢?

还可以。

不错。

早上好。

晚上好。

晚安。

你几岁?

你今年多大?

我二十五岁。

你是哪里人?

我是英国人。

你对澳大利亚的印象
如何?

我是第一次来中国。

我想学一些中文。

今天天气挺好。

哎呀，雨下得真大!

你知道明天的天气预
报吗?

天气预报说明天会
冷。

明天可能下雨。

Chinese Names

Most Chinese names consist of two or three characters, or words, with the first being the surname. If a person is called Wang Zhonghua, for example, "Wang" is his family name and "Zhonghua" his given name. In Chinese culture, to call someone by his given name is a privilege reserved for family members and close friends. Therefore, to address someone politely, you should use either the full name, such as Wang Zhonghua, or the surname plus a title, such as *Wang Lǎoshī* (Teacher Wang).

In informal situations, Chinese call each other by their last names preceded by *xiǎo* (young) or *lǎo* (old). For example, if Wang Zhonghua was a young man, he would be called Xiao Wang.

If the other person is not very familiar, Chinese often use the address *xiānsheng* (Mr.) or *nǚshì* (Ms.). In crowded stores, you will even hear the salesclerk being called *shīfu*, in hopes of faster service.

(Psst... What'll I Call Him?)

If your friend's last name is Wang, how should you address him or her? Here are some suggestions for you to choose from, depending on Wang's age and status.

Continued

Talk About Family

Are you married?	*Nǐ jiéhūn le ma?*
Yes (I'm married).	*Jié le.*
No, not yet.	*Méi yǒu.*
I have (one) child.	*Wǒ yǒu (yí) gè háizi.*
Boy or girl?	*Shì nánháir háishì nǚháir?*
How old?	*Jǐ suì le?*
Do you have (brothers and sisters)?	*Nǐ yǒu (xiōngdì jiěmèi) ma?*
I have one (older sister).	*Wǒ yǒu yí gè (jiějie).*
Who are the members of your family?	*Nǐ jiā dōu yǒu shénme rén?*

Talk About Work

What do you do?	*Nǐ zuò shénme gōngzuò?*
I'm a (teacher).	*Wǒ shì (jiàoshī).*
Where do you (teach)?	*Nǐ zài nǎi (jiāoshū)?*
Are you satisfied with your (work)?	*Xǐhuan nǐde (gōngzuò) ma?*
It's not bad.	*Hái kěyǐ.*
I like (my work) very much.	*Wǒ fēicháng xǐhuan (wǒde) gōngzuò.*
I'm considering (changing jobs).	*Wǒ zhèngzài kǎolù(diào gōngzuò) ne.*
I'm not very (satisfied).	*Bú tài (mǎnyì).*

Talk About Hobbies

What do you usually do in (your spare time)?	*Nǐ (yèyú shíjiān) gàn shénme?*

你结婚了吗?

结了。

没有。

我有一个孩子。

是男孩还是女孩?

几岁了?

你有兄弟姐妹吗?

我有一个姐姐。

你家都有什么人?

你做什么工作?

我是教师。

你在哪教书?

喜欢你的工作吗?

还可以。

我非常喜欢我的工作。

我正在考虑调工作呢。

不太满意。

你业余时间干什么?

elderly man	*Wang yéye*
elderly woman	*Wang nǎinai*
older person	*Lǎo Wang*
business or professional	
man	*Wang xiānsheng*
woman	*Wang nǚshì*
(Mrs.)	*Wang fūrén*
(Miss)	*Wang xiǎojiě*
young person	*Xiǎo Wang*
Driver	*Wang shīfu*
Bureau Director	*Wang júzhǎng*
School Principal	*Wang xiàozhǎng*
Manager	*Wang jīnglǐ*

Chinese Idioms

There are many four-word idioms in Chinese known as *chéngyǔ* (set phrase), which are sayings originating from folk stories. Because each *chéngyǔ* is a concise way of conveying a poignant meaning, Chinese use them often in everyday conversation. When the situation is ripe, delight your friends with these favorites.

老马识途	*Lǎo mǎ shí tú* (old horse knows road) Let experience take over.
熟能生巧	*Shú néng shēng qiǎo* (mature ability brings skill) Practice makes perfect.
亡羊补牢	*Wáng yáng bǔ láo* (lost sheep mend fold) Making repairs after the damage: better late than never.
掩耳盗铃	*Yǎn ěr dào líng* (cover ears steal bell) You're only fooling yourself.

Continued

49

FRIENDS

I usually (read books). | *Wǒ jīngcháng (kàn shū).*

I like to (play soccer). | *Wǒ xǐhuan (tī zúqiú).*

What are you most (interested in)? | *Nǐ zuì (gǎnxìngqù) de shì shén me?*

I'm especially interested in (music). | *Wǒ duì (yīnyuè) tèbié gǎnxìng qù.*

Talk About Politics

Are you satisfied with China's present (economic) policy? | *Nǐ duì zhōngguó mùqián de (jīngjì) zhèngcè mǎnyì ma?*

What areas are currently undergoing reform? | *Mùqián yǒu nǎxiē lǐngyù zài shíxíng gǎigé?*

Do you think China's present (rural) reform is making progress? | *Nǐ rènwéi Zhōngguó mùqián de (nóngcūn) gǎigé qǔdé jìnzhǎn le ma?*

Do most Chinese join the (Communist Party of China)? | *Shìfǒu dàduōshù Zhōngguórén dōu jiārù (Zhōngguó Gòngchǎn dǎng)?*

Out of every ten (young people) how many are [Party members]? | *Měi shí gè (niánqīng rén) zhōng yǒu jǐ gè shì [Dǎngyuán]?*

Does (everyone) take part in elections? | *(Měigè rén) dōu cānjiā xuǎnjǔ ma?*

What do you think of (American) foreign policy? | *Nǐ duì (Měiguó) de wàijiāo zhèngcè zěnme kàn?*

Saying Good-bye

I'm very pleased to have met you. | *Rènshi nǐ hěn gāoxìng.*

It's been nice talking with you. | *Hěn gāoxìng néng hé nǐ jiāotán.*

Good-bye. (See you again.) | *Zàijiàn.*

我经常看书。

我喜欢踢足球。

你最感兴趣的是什么?

我对音乐特别感兴趣。

你对中国目前的(经济)政策满意吗?

目前有哪些领域在实行改革?

你认为中国目前的农村改革取得进展了吗?

是否大多数中国人都加入中国共产党?

每十个年轻人中有几个是党员?

每个人都参加选举吗?

你对美国的外交政策怎么看?

认识你很高兴。

很高兴能和你交谈。

再见。

一箭双雕	*Yí jiàn shuāng diāo* (one arrow two hawks) Killing two birds with one stone.

Seeing Off a Friend

It is an age-old custom in China to see friends to the gate when they leave one's home. Many classic poems, in fact, describe the sadness of that moment of final parting. Here are some phrases that are still used when a guest leaves.

Wǒ sòng sòng nǐ.	Let me see you off.
Bú sòng bú sòng.	No, no, it's not necessary.
Méi guānxi méi guānxi.	It's nothing, don't worry.
Qǐng liúbù.	Please don't trouble —this is far enough.
Shù bù yuǎn sòng.	All right, pardon my not seeing you out farther.

What You'll Hear

bù hǎoyìsi	feel embarrassed
Bú jiàn bú sàn.	I'll be there. Don't leave without me.
Chōuyān ma?	Do you smoke?
gòuqiàng	not likely
Hǎojiǔ bú jiàn.	Long time no see.
huānyíng	welcome
Jiùshì!	Precisely!
Jiù zhèyàng ba.	That's settled, then.
Zāo gāo le.	It's a disaster.
Zěnme huí shì(r)?	What happened here?

Signs

jiǎng wénmíng
Be Civilized

jiǎng lǐmào
Be Polite

jiǎng wèishēng
Be Cleanly

jiǎng jìlǜ
Be Orderly

jiǎng dàodé
Be Moral

六 liù **6 Food**

Wèidao hǎo jí le!
Delicious!

Hungry? Need a quick pickup? Dying for a hamburger? Not to worry—China offers some of the best food in the world, if only you know where to find it and how to ask for it. You can find food on the train, in the hotel, at a snack stall, and, of course, in a restaurant. Whether you're buying a bowl of noodles or ordering a twenty-course banquet, the phrases in this chapter will help you make clear what you want.

FOOD

Eating on the Run

I'm thirsty.	*Wǒ kě le.*
I'm hungry.	*Wǒ è le.*
I'm starving.	*Wǒ è sǐ le.*
Where can I get something to eat?	*Nǎr yǒu mài chī de?*
Where can I buy a (cold drink)?	*Nǎr mài (lěngyǐn)?*
(Two) bottles of [beer], please.	*Qǐng lái (liǎng) píng [píjiǔ].*
I'd like a cup of (coffee).	*Wǒ yào yì bēi (kāfēi).*
Please give me a bowl of (noodles).	*Qǐng lái yì wǎn (miàntiáo).*
How much is this?	*Zhège duōshao qián?*
Give me (one), please.	*Qǐng gěi wǒ (yí) gè.*
Can I have a doggie bag, please?	*Wǒ kěyǐ dǎbāo ma?*
Do I need to return the (bottle)?	*Yào tuì (píng) ma?*
I'm leaving the (bowl) here.	*Wǒ bǎ (wǎn) fàng zài zhèr.*
Do I get back a (deposit)?	*Yǒu (yājīn) ma?*

Finding a Place to Eat

Where is there a good (restaurant)?	*Nǎr yǒu hǎo yìdiǎn de (fànguǎn)?*
Is it (expensive)?	*Guì (bú) guì?*
I would like to go to a (Sichuan) restaurant.	*Wǒ xiǎng qù yì jiā (Sìchuān) cāntīng.*
We would like a simple meal.	*Wǒmen xiǎng chī jiǎndān yìdiǎn.*
I'm dying for a (Western meal).	*Wǒ fēicháng xiǎng chī (Xīcān).*
There's a (fast-food place) nearby.	*Fùjìn yǒu yì jiā (kuàicān diàn).*
Let's go.	*Zǒu ba.*

54

What's for Breakfast?

Chinese rarely have bacon and eggs for breakfast. Instead, they have a bowl of hot rice porridge (congee) with a few pickled vegetables or other side dishes. On the run, instead of a doughnut and coffee, Chinese have *yóutiáo* (fried cruller) and *dòujiāng* (soybean milk). If you'd like to try breakfast Chinese-style, ask a local friend where to find these favorite items:

我渴了。
我饿了。
我饿死了。
哪儿有卖吃的?

哪儿卖冷饮?
请来两瓶啤酒。
我要一杯咖啡。
请来一碗面条。

这个多少钱?
请给我一个。
我可以打包吗?

要退瓶吗?
我把碗放在这儿。
有押金吗?

哪儿有好一点的饭馆?

贵不贵?
我想去一家四川餐厅。

我们想吃简单一点。
我非常想吃西餐。
附近有一家快餐店。

走吧!

包子	bāozi steamed dumpling
大米粥	dàmǐzhōu rice porridge (congee)
豆浆	dòujiāng soybean milk
豆沙包	dòushābāo steamed bean-paste dumpling
煎饼	jiānbǐng crepe (with cruller)
泡菜	pàocài pickled vegetables
肉松	ròusōng shredded dried meat
烧饼	shāobǐng sesame seed biscuit
汤面	tāngmiàn soup noodles
咸鸭蛋	xián yādàn salted duck egg
油条	yóutiáo fried cruller (twisted fried bread stick)
榨菜	zhàcài hot pickled mustard
炸糕	zhágāo fried sticky-rice cake

Making Reservations

I'd like to make a reservation for (Tuesday) night.	*Wǒ xiǎng yùdìng (xīngqī èr) wǎn shang de fàn.*
We'll arrive at (7:30).	*Wǒmen (qī diǎn bàn) lái.*
There will be (four) people.	*(Sì) gè rén.*
I'd like to pay (forty) yuan per person.	*Měi rén (sì shí) yuán.*
Will you be able to accommodate us?	*Nǐmen néng jiēdài ma?*
What time would be better?	*Shénme shíjiān jiào hǎo?*
How much is it per person?	*Měi rén duōshao qián?*
Are beverages included?	*Bāokuò yǐnliào ma?*
Is there anything (cheaper)?	*Yǒu (piányi yìdiǎn) de ma?*
Okay, that'll do.	*Hǎo, jiù zhèyàng.*
See you (Tuesday).	*(Xīngqī èr) jiàn.*

Getting a Table

A party of (three).	*Wǒmen (sān) gè rén.*
A table for (two), please.	*(Liǎng) gè rén, zuò nǎr?*
There's a draft here.	*Zhèr yǒu fēng.*
Could we switch to another table?	*Néng huàn gè zhuōzi ma?*
May we sit over there?	*Néng zuò zài nàr ma?*

What's for Dinner?

You've finally found a place to eat. You are seated at the table, and the waiter has handed you the menu. Now what? If you are puzzled by the menu at hand, try pointing to some of the choices below and asking *Yǒu méi yǒu zhège* (Do you have this?) The items here are standard dishes available at most restaurants.

我想预定星期二晚上的饭。

我们七点半来。

四个人。

每人四十元。

你们能接待吗?

什么时间较好?

每人多少钱?

包括饮料吗?

有便宜一点的吗?

好,就这样。

(星期二)见。

我们三个人。

两个人,坐哪儿?

这儿有风。

能换个桌子吗?

能坐在那儿吗?

香酥鸡	xiāngsūjī crispy fried chicken
宫保鸡丁	gōngbǎo jīdīng hot spicy chicken with peanuts
糖醋鱼	tángcù yú sweet-and-sour fish
红烧鱼	hóngshāo yú braised fish in brown sauce
木须肉	mùxu ròu mushu pork
鱼香肉丝	yúxiāng ròusī pork in hot garlic sauce
葱头炒牛肉	cōngtóu chǎo níuròu beef with onions
麻婆豆腐	mápó dòufu hot spicy beancurd
砂锅豆腐	shāguō dòufu beancurd casserole
香菇冬笋	xiānggū dōngsǔn black mushrooms and bamboo shoots
香菇菜心	xiānggu càixīn Chinese cabbage with mushrooms
炒豆芽	chǎo dòuyá sauteed bean sprouts
酸辣汤	suānlà tāng hot-and-sour soup
米饭	mǐfàn rice
馒头	mántou steamed roll

FOOD

Ordering

Waiter/waitress!	*Fúwùyuán!*
The menu, please.	*Qǐng gěi wǒmen càidān.*
What is the house specialty?	*Zhèr yǒu shénme tèsè cài?*
What regional cuisine do you serve here?	*Zhèr yǒu shénme fēngwèi cài?*
Do you have (Beijing Duck)?	*Yǒu (Běijīng kǎoyā) ma?*
Can you recommend some dishes?	*Nǐ néng tuījiàn yìxiē cài ma?*
I like (chicken).	*Wǒ xǐhuan chī (jī).*
My favorite food is (shrimp).	*Wǒ zuì ài chī (xiā).*
I don't like (mushrooms).	*Wǒ bù xǐhuan (mógu).*
I don't eat (pork).	*Wǒ bù chī (zhūròu).*
I'm vegetarian.	*Wǒ zhǐ chī sùcài.*
I'm allergic to (seafood).	*Wǒ chī (hǎixiān) huì guòmǐn.*
Please order more (vegetables).	*Qǐng duō lái jǐ pán (shūcài).*
What (soups) do you have?	*Yǒu shénme (tāng)?*
Is the (fish) fresh?	*(Yú) xīnxiān ma?*
Please leave out the (MSG).	*Qǐng bú yào fàng (wèijīng).*
Please don't make it too (spicy).	*Bú yào tài (là).*
May I order now?	*Kěyǐ diǎncài le ma?*
I'll have...	*Wǒ yào...*
one (homestyle beancurd)	*yí gè (jiācháng dòufu)*
(two) bowls of rice	*(liǎng) wǎn mǐfàn*
a pot of (jasmine) tea	*yì hú (mòlìhuā) chá*

服务员！

请给我们菜单。

这儿有什么特色菜？

这儿有什么风味菜？

有北京烤鸭吗？

你能推荐一些菜吗？

我喜欢吃鸡。

我最爱吃虾。

我不喜欢蘑菇。

我不吃猪肉。

我只吃素菜。

我吃海鲜会过敏。

请多来几盘蔬菜。

有什么汤？

鱼新鲜吗？

请不要放味精。

不要太辣。

可以点菜了吗？

我要……

　　一个家常豆腐

　　两碗米饭

　　一壶茉莉花茶。

Local Snacks

As you travel throughout China, you will have the chance to sample many local snacks. Below are some of the most popular snacks in four major cities.

Beijing

冰糖葫芦	*bīngtáng húlu*
	candied haws on a stick
涮羊肉	*shuànyángròu*
	Mongolian hot pot
豌豆黄	*wāndòuhuáng*
	pea-flour cake
杏仁茶	*xìngrénchá*
	almond-flour tea
羊肉串	*yángròuchuàn*
	mutton shish kebab

Shanghai

豆沙包	*dòushābāo*
	sweet bean-paste dumplings
馄饨	*húndùn*
	wontons
小笼包	*xiǎolóngbāo*
	small steamed dumplings
芝麻汤团	*zhīma tāngtuán*
	sweet sesame-paste dumplings in soup

Xi'an

饸饹	*héle*
	buckwheat spaghetti
面皮	*miànpi*
	flat noodles made of steamed refined wheat dough, served with sauces and seasonings
柿子饼	*shìzibǐng*
	fried persimmon cake
羊肉泡馍	*yángròu pàomó*
	crumbled unleavened bread soaked in lamb stew

During the Meal

That's not what I ordered.	*Zhè bú shì wǒ diǎn de cài.*
I asked for (curried chicken).	*Wǒ yào de shì (gālí jī).*
This is too (salty).	*Zhège tài (xián) le.*
This is not (fresh).	*Zhège bù (xīnxiān).*
The food is (cold).	*Cài (liáng) le.*
What (meat) is this?	*Zhè shì shénme (ròu)?*
May we have some (forks)?	*Néng gěi wǒmen jǐbǎ (chāzi) ma?*
Do you have any (hot sauce)?	*Yǒu (làjiàng) ma?*
We need some (napkins).	*Wǒmen yào (cānjīnzhǐ).*
This dish is (excellent).	*Zhège cài (hǎochī jí le).*
Can you write down the (name of the dish) for me?	*Nǐ néng bāng wǒ xiě xià (cài míng) ma?*

Ending the Meal

We have finished.	*Chī wán le.*
Check, please.	*Jiézhàng ba.*
That was a (very good) meal.	*Zhè dùn fàn chī de (hěn hǎo).*
We enjoyed it.	*Wǒmen hěn mǎnyì.*

这不是我点的菜。

我要的是咖喱鸡。

这个太咸了。

这个不新鲜。

菜凉了。

这是什么肉？

能给我们几把叉子吗？

有辣酱吗？

我们要餐巾纸。

这个菜好吃极了。

你能帮我写下菜名吗？

吃完了。

结帐吧。

这顿饭吃得很好。

我们很满意。

Guangzhou

春卷	*chūnjuǎn (chun kuen)*	spring roll
烧麦	*shāomai (siu mai)*	steamed pork dumplings
虾饺	*xiājiǎo (ha kaau)*	shrimp dumplings
鲜荷叶饭	*xiān héyè fàn (sin haw mai faan)*	rice wrapped in fresh lotus leaf
炸虾球	*zháxiāqiú (cha ha kow)*	fried shrimp balls

● Cantonese pronunciations are in parentheses.

What You'll Hear

Gānbēi!	Cheers! Bottoms up.
Hái yào shénme?	Would you like anything else?
Jǐ wèi?	How many people?
Nǐmen xiǎng hē shénme?	What would you like to drink?
Nǐmen yùdìng le ma?	Do you have a reservation?
Qǐng jiézhàng.	Please pay the bill.
Yào mǐfàn ma?	Do you want rice?
Zhù nǐ jiànkāng!	To your health!

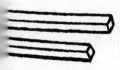

Signs

cāntīng
Dining Hall, Restaurant

léngyǐn rèyǐn
Cold and Hot Drinks

yān jiǔ shípǐn
Cigarettes, Liquor, Wine, Foodstuffs

shuǐjiǎo
Boiled Dumplings

miàntiáo
Noodles

七 qī 7 Sightseeing

Tài bàng le!
Wow! Too much!

China abounds with scenic, historic, and cultural attractions, as well as factories and schools to visit. You will have questions to ask and comments to make at each site. Whether seeking facts or simply asking someone to move aside for a photograph, it will be invaluable to know a few words of Chinese.

SIGHTSEEING

Planning Your Excursion

Can you tell me where the (China International Travel Service) is?

Nǐ néng gàosù wǒ (Zhōngguó Guójì Lǚxíngshè) zài nǎr ma?

I need an English-speaking (guide).

Wǒ xūyào yí gè yīngyǔ (dǎoyóu).

What will be the fee per (hour)?

Měi (xiǎoshí) duōshao qián?

Can you arrange a trip to (Xi'an)?

Néng ānpái dào (Xī'ān) lǚxíng ma?

Can you recommend a (sightseeing tour)?

Néng tuījiàn yì tiáo (guānguāng lùxiàn) ma?

I want to see some (scenic spots).

Wǒ xiǎng kàn yìxiē (fēngjǐng diǎn).

I would like to visit a (factory).

Wǒ xiǎng cānguān yí gè (gōngchǎng).

Do you have a (local) map?

Yǒu (dāngdì) dìtú ma?

What are the (places of interest) in this city?

Zhèige chéngshì yǒu shénme (kě kàn de dìfang)?

What is the itinerary?

Rìchéng shì zěnme ānpái de?

Are we going by (bus)?

Shì zuò (qìchē) qù ma?

How long will the ride be?

Zuò chē yào duōjiǔ?

When do we set out?

Shénme shíhou chūfā?

At the Site

What (park) is this?

Zhè shì shénme (gōngyuán)?

When was this (palace) built?

Zhèige (gōngdiàn) shì shénme shíhou jiàn de?

你能告诉我中国国际旅行社在哪儿吗?

我需要一个英语导游。

每小时多少钱?

能安排到西安旅行吗?

能推荐一条观光路线吗?

我想看一些风景点。

我想参观一个工厂。

有当地地图吗?

这个城市有什么可看的地方?

日程是怎么安排的?

是坐汽车去吗?

坐车要多久?

什么时候出发?

这是什么公园?

这个宫殿是什么时候建的?

Symbols

Chinese art is full of symbolic images–you will often see dragons, or peaches, or plum blossoms on paintings, architecture, textiles, and decorative objects. What do these motifs stand for? Below are some of the traditional symbols and their meanings.

bat: luck
chrysanthemum: nobility, purity
crane: longevity
dragon: the emperor, China
lion: power, dignity
lotus: purity, continuity
mandarin ducks: marital harmony
peach: long life, immortality
peony: wealth, honor
phoenix: the empress
pine tree: longevity
plum blossom: transience, delicacy
tiger: guardian against evil
tortoise: longevity

Flowers

China's vast territory extends across the frigid, temperate, and tropical zones, making it possible for a great variety of plant species. Below are the names of some common flowers in China. Use this list when asking a local friend *zhè shì shénmè huā* (What flower is this?):

茶花	*cháhuā*	camellia
杜鹃花	*dùjuānhuā*	azalea
凤仙花	*fèngxiānhuā*	touch-me-not
桂花	*guìhuā*	cassia

continued

SIGHTSEEING

How large is (Tian'anmen Square)?	(Tiān ānmén)Guǎngchǎng duōdà?
How high is this (pagoda)?	Zhèige (tǎ) duōgāo?
What does this (lion) symbolize?	Zhèige (shīzi) dàibiǎo shénme?
Whom does this picture portray?	Zhèi zhāng huà huà de shì shuí?
What other (temples) can I visit?	Hái yǒu shénme (sìmiào) kě kàn?
How long will we stay here?	Wǒmen yào zài zhèr dāi duōjiǔ?
I want to buy some (souvenirs).	Wǒ xiǎng mǎi yìxiē (jìniàn pǐn).

At the Zoo

I would like to see the (giant pandas).	Wǒ xiǎng kàn (dàxióngmāo).
Where is its habitat?	Tā zhù zài shénme dìfang?
What does (it) eat?	(Tā) chī shénme?
How many cubs does the (panda) have in one brood?	(Xióngmāo) yì tāi shēng jǐge?
How old is this (panda)?	Zhèizhī (xióngmāo) duōdà le?

At the Factory

May I ask a few questions?	Wǒ kěyǐ wèn jǐge wèntí ma?
What are your products?	Nǐmen yǒu shénme chǎnpǐn?
How many (workers) do you have?	Nǐmen yǒu duōshao (gōngrén)?
How long does it take to complete (one carpet)?	Zuò (yí kuài dìtǎn) yào duō cháng shíjiān?

天安门广场多大？

这个塔多高？

这个狮子代表什么？

这张画画的是谁？

还有什么寺庙可看？

我们要在这儿呆多久？

我想买一些纪念品。

我想看大熊猫。

它住在什么地方？

它吃什么？

熊猫一胎生几个？

这只熊猫多大了？

我可以问几个问题吗？

你们有什么产品？

你们有多少工人？

做一块地毯要多长时间？

荷花	héhuā	lotus
鸡冠花	jīguānhuā	cock's comb
夹竹桃	jiāzhútáo	oleander
腊梅	làméi	wintersweet
兰花	lánhuā	orchid
茉莉	mòli	jasmine
牡丹	mǔdan	tree peony
蔷薇	qiángwēi	hedge rose
秋海棠	qiūhǎitáng	begonia
芍药	sháoyao	peony
水浮莲	shuǐfúlián	water lily
水仙	shuǐxiān	narcissus
绣球	xiùqiú	geranium
月季	yuèjì	Chinese rose

Trees

China observes arbor day on March 12, when young trees are planted all across the country. In southern towns, shade trees often line both sides of the streets, providing refuge from the summer heat. When identifying the trees you see, refer to the list below:

白果树	báiguǒshù	gingko
白杨树	báiyángshù	aspen
柏树	bǎishù	cypress
松树	sōngshù	pine
丁香树	dīngxiāngshù	lilac
核桃树	hétaoshù	walnut
槐树	huáishù	locust
柳树	Liǔshù	willow
榕树	róngshù	banyan
桑树	sāngshù	mulberry
石榴树	shíliushù	pomegranate
柿子树	shìzishù	persimmon

continued

How long did you train for this job?	Nǐ xué guò duōjiǔ?
Do you have a (labor union)?	Nǐmen yǒu (gōnghuì) ma?
Do you use a (bonus system)?	Nǐmen yǒu (jiǎngjīn zhìdù) ma?
What is the monthly salary of a (worker)?	(Gōngrén) měi yuè gōngzī duōshao?
What are your working hours?	Nǐmen měi tiān jǐdiǎn shàngxià bān?
What is your work quota per (day)?	Měi (tiān) de gōngzuòliàng shì duōshao?

Taking a Photo

Can I take a picture here?	Néng zài zhèr zhàoxiàng ma?
Do you mind if I photograph you?	Kěyǐ gěi nǐ zhào zhāng xiàng ma?
Would you take a picture for me, please?	Nǐ néng tì wǒ zhào zhāng xiàng ma?
Everything is set.	Dōu tiáo hǎo le.
Just press the button.	Zhǐ yào àn kuàimén jiù xíng le.
Excuse me, please move aside.	Duìbuqǐ, qǐng ràng yíxià.
We want to take a picture here.	Wǒmen xiǎng zài zhèr zhào zhāng xiàng.
Please give me your address.	Qǐng gěi wǒ nǐde dìzhǐ.
I'll send you (the photos) later.	Yǐhòu wǒ bǎ (zhàopiàn) gěi nǐ jì qù.

你学过多久?

你们有工会吗?

你们有奖金制度吗?

工人每月工资多少?

你们每天几点上下班?

每天的工作量是多少?

桃树	*táoshù*	peach
梧桐树	*wútóngshù*	Chinese parasol
柚子树	*yòuzishù*	pomelo
榆树	*yúshù*	elm
樟树	*zhāngshù*	camphor

Zoo Animals

When you visit zoos in China, you will see a few animals that are not often found in Western zoos. The all-time favorite, of course, is the giant panda. Here are the names of some animals particular to China.

大熊猫	*dàxióngmāo*	giant panda
丹顶鹤	*dāndǐnghè*	red-crowned crane
金丝猴	*jīnsīhóu*	golden-haired monkey
滩羊	*tānyáng*	argali sheep
小熊猫	*xiǎoxióngmāo*	lesser panda

能在这儿照相吗?

可以给你照张相吗?

你能替我照张相吗?

都调好了。

只要按快门就行了。

对不起,请让一下。

我们想在这儿照张相。

请给我你的地址。

以后我把照片给你寄去。

What You'll Hear

Dōu dào le.	We're all here.
Guānmén Le.	It's closed.
Jīntiān xiūxi.	Today is the day off.
lǎowài	foreigner (slang)
ménpiào	admission ticket
míngxìnpiàn	postcard
wàibīn	foreign guest
wàiguórén	foreigner
Xiǎoxīn!	Careful!
Yánjìn pāizhào.	Photography prohibited.

Signs

huānyíng
Welcome

shòu piào chù
Ticket Office

ménpiào: 2 yuan
Admission: 2 yuan

bù zhǔn suídì tùtán
No Spitting

yóukè zhǐbù
Visitors Keep Out

八 **8** Shopping
bā

> *Duōshao qián?*
> How much?

Shopping in China outside the Friendship Stores and other shops catering to foreign tourists is like treasure-hunting in a jungle. The hunt will be much easier if you can describe what you want.

In the many free markets that have sprung up all over China, the key phrase after *Duōshao qián?* (How much?) is *Tài guì le* (too expensive). In nongovernmental stores, especially high-priced souvenir shops, you can try *Néng piányì diǎn ma?* (Can the price be lowered?) Then be prepared to bargain!

SHOPPING

Scouting the Market

Where can I buy some souvenirs? — *Nǎli kěyǐ mǎi dào jìniànpǐn ne?*

Where is the nearest (arts and crafts store)? — *Zuìjìn de (gōngyì měishù shāngdiàn) zài nǎr?*

Can you recommend a (department store)? — *Nǐ néng jièshào yí gè (bǎihuò shāngdiàn) ma?*

I would like to buy some (silk fabric). — *Wǒ xiǎng mǎi diǎn (sīchóu).*

Can you accompany me to the (free market)? — *Nǐ néng péi wǒ qù (zìyóu shìchǎng) ma?*

When does it open? — *Shénme shíhou kāimén?*

Making the Find

Can you help me? — *Qǐng bāng yíxià máng.*

I'd like to take a look at this (jacket). — *Wǒ xiǎng kàn yíxià zhèi jiàn (jiākè shān).*

Do you have any (others)? — *Yǒu (qítā) de ma?*

I'm looking for (cloisonne vases). — *Wǒ xiǎng mǎi (jǐngtàilán huā píng).*

This has a (flaw). — *Zhèige yǒu (máobìng).*

Please show me (that one). — *Qǐng gěi wǒ (nèige) kànkan.*

Is this (handmade)? — *Zhè shì (shǒugōng zuò de) ma?*

What kind of fabric is this? — *Zhè shì shénme liàozi de?*

Where is it made? — *Nǎr chǎn de?*

How much is it? — *Duōshao qián?*

Can you bring the price down? — *Néng piányi diǎn ma?*

72

哪里可以买到纪念品
呢？

最近的工艺美术商店
在哪儿？

你能介绍一个百货商
店吗？

我想买点丝绸。

你能陪我去自由市场
吗？

什么时候开门？

请帮一下忙。

我想看一下这件夹克
衫。

有其他的吗？

我想买景泰蓝花瓶。

这个有毛病。

请给我那个看看。

这是手工做的吗？

这是什么料子的？

哪儿产的？

多少钱？

能便宜点吗？

Cashier's Booth

Many local stores have a cashier's booth where you must pay for your purchase before picking it up at the sales counter. When you have decided what to buy, the salesclerk at the counter will write out a bill and give you two copies. Take those copies to the cashier's booth, pay the amount shown, and return with a stamped copy of the bill as your receipt. When you hand the receipt to the salesclerk, he or she will give you your goods.

Special Items

The true shopper cannot be deterred, language barrier or not. If you wish to buy a few special Chinese items but have difficulty telling the store clerk what you want, try pointing to the list below. (Refer to the dictionary section for pronunciations.)

竹编	bamboo ware (woven)
蜡染	batik
织锦	brocade
中山装	cadre's jacket
毛笔	calligraphy brush
地毯	carpet
开士米毛衣	cashmere sweater
旗袍	cheongsam (gown)
图章	chop (seal)
泥人	clay figurine
景泰蓝	cloisonne
棉衣	cotton-padded jacket
棉鞋	cotton-padded shoes
双面绣	double-sided embroidery
折扇	folding fan

Continued

Closing the Deal

Okay, I'll take it.

Hǎo, jiù yào tā.

It's too expensive.

Tài guì le.

Can you give me a discount?

Kěyǐ dǎ zhé ma?

I don't want it.

Wǒ bú yào.

Could you wrap it for me, please?

Qǐng bāo yíxià, hǎo ma?

Please wrap each separately.

Qǐng fēn kāi bāo.

Do you have a (box) for it?

Yǒu (hézi) ma?

Please give me (a receipt).

Qǐng gěi wǒ (fāpiào).

Art and Antiques

Is this an (original)?

Zhè shì (yuánzuò) ma?

Is the (calligrapher) still living?

Zhèige (shūfǎjiā) hái huózhe ma?

Would you write down the artist's (brief background)?

Néng bǎ zhèige yìshùjiā de (jiǎndān qíngkuàng) xiě gěi wǒ ma?

Do you sell (reproductions)?

Zhèr mài (fùzhìpǐn) ma?

When was this made?

Zhè shì shénme niándài de?

What dynasty does it date from?

Tā shì nǎge cháodài de?

I must have one with a red wax seal on it.

Wǒ yào yí gè dǎguò huǒqī yìn de.

I won't be able to take this (out of the country).

Zhèige wǒ bù néng dài (chū jìng).

Books

I'm looking for a (good) English-Chinese dictionary.

Wǒ xiǎng mǎi yì běn (hǎo) de Yīng-Hàn zìdiǎn.

皮帽子	fur hat
砚台	ink slab
墨	ink stick
铁花	iron openwork
玉雕	jade carving
漆器	lacquerware
瓷器	porcelain
军帽	Mao cap
军便服	Mao jacket
鼻烟壶	miniature bottle painting
微雕	miniature carving
剪纸	papercut
珍珠霜	pearl cream
印泥	red paste for seals
宣纸	Xuan paper
檀香扇	sandalwood fan
皮影	shadow puppet
贝雕画	shell mosaic
丝绸	silk fabric
丝绸睡袍	silk robe
拓片	stone rubbings
壁毯	tapestry
清凉油	tiger balm
鸭舌帽	worker's cap

好，就要它。

太贵了。

可以打折吗？

我不要。

请包一下好吗？

请分开包。

有盒子吗？

请给我发票。

这是原作吗？

这个书法家还活着吗？

能把这个艺术家的简单情况写给我吗？

这儿卖复制品吗？

这是什么年代的？

它是哪个朝代的？

我要一个打过火漆印的。

这个我不能带出境。

我想买一本好的英汉字典。

Buying Jade

The main factors that go into the price of a piece of jade are the material used, the carving skill, and the color. In the Chinese jade industry, the materials are grouped into three categories. They are:

féicuì 翡翠

Jadeite. The most valuable jade, its color appears green but on close inspection can be seen to have both white and green elements.

continued

75

Where are the (children's) books?	(Értóng) shū zài nǎr?
I'm looking for a book about Chinese (youth).	Wǒ xiǎng mǎi yì běn guānyú zhōngguó (qīngnián) de shū.
I'm looking for works by (Lu Xun).	Wǒ xiǎng mǎi (Lǔ Xùn) de zuòpǐn.
Do you have (this book)?	Yǒu (zhè běn shū) ma?

Clothing

Can I try it on?	Néng shì yíxià ma?
Do you have a (large)?	Yǒu (dà hào) de ma?
Is there a (mirror)?	Yǒu (jìngzi) ma?
Please show me a (smaller) one.	Yǒu (xiǎo yìdiǎn) de ma?
I'd like something (brighter).	Wǒ xǐhuan (yánsè xiānyàn yìdiǎn) de.
I wear size (42).	Wǒ chuān (sìshí èr) hào.
This pair of pants doesn't fit me.	Zhè tiáo chángkù bù hé shēn.
It is little (loose) around the waist.	Yāo bù sōng le yìxiē.
May I see some others in different colors?	Wǒ kěyǐ kàn qítā bùtóng yánsè de ma?
Will this sweater shrink any when washed?	Zhè jiàn máoyī xǐ le huì bú huì suōshuǐ?

Film

I'd like to buy an automatic camera.	Wǒ xiǎng mǎi jià quán zìdòng zhàoxiàngjī.
I'd like (two) rolls of [color-print film].	Wǒ xiǎng mǎi (liǎng) gè [cǎijuǎn].
(36) exposures	(Sānshí liù) zhāng de

儿童书在哪儿？

我想买一本关于中国青年的书。

我想买鲁迅的作品。

有这本书吗？

能试一下吗？

有大号的吗？

有镜子吗？

有小一点的吗？

我喜欢颜色鲜艳一点的。

我穿42号。

这条长裤不合身。

腰部松了一些。

我可以看其他不同颜色的吗？

这件毛衣洗了会不会缩水？

我想买架全自动照相机。

我想买两个彩卷。

36张的

mǎnǎo 玛瑙
Agate. The second most valuable, it is semi-transparent. Most agate pieces are red, white, or the two colors mixed.

xiùyù 岫玉 (and others)
Manchurian jasper. A serpentine, this stone is used in the less expensive jade pieces. This third category also includes other materials, such as crystals.

How to Bargain

You're at a free market. You see the perfect cotton vest to bring home for a souvenir. But the vendor is sharp—you know he's out to scalp you, how do you bring the price down? It takes creative thinking and determination. (B is the buyer, and V is the vendor).

B: *Zhèi jiàn mián bèixīn duōshao qián?*
How much is this cotton vest?

V: *Shí kuài qián.*
Ten yuan.

B: *Shénme! Kāi wánxiào. Shí kuài qián! Tài guì le! Wǔ kuài zěnmeyàng?*
What? You've got to be kidding. Ten yuan! Too much! How's five yuan?

V: *Bù xíng, bù xíng. Gěi jiǔ kuài qián ba.*
No way, no way. Give me nine, then.

B: *Jiǔ kuài! Bú yào. Nǐ zhèi jiàn bèixīn zhìliàng bù hǎo. Zuìduō gěinǐ qī kuài.*
Nine yuan! I don't want it. The quality of this vest is not very good. The most I'll offer is seven yuan.

V: *Qī kuài! Zài jiā yìdiǎn ba.*
Seven yuan! Come on, raise it a little.

B: *Hǎo Le, hǎc Le. Gěi nǐ qī kuài wǔ ba.*
Okay, okay. I'll give you seven and a half.

continued

(135) mm	(yāo sān wǔ) de
(100) ASA	(yìbǎi) dù de
I'd like (Kodak) film.	Wǒ xiǎng yào (Kēdá) jiāojuǎn.
Where can I have (slides) processed?	Nǎr néng chōng (fǎnzhuǎn piàn)?
I'd like to have this film (developed).	Wǒ yào (chōng) jiāojuǎn.
Please do not (make prints).	Bú yào (kuòyìn).
I'd like to (order reprints).	Wǒ xiǎng (jiāyìn jǐ zhāng).
Please print (one) of this.	Zhèige qǐng yìn (yì) zhāng.
Please use (Fuji) paper.	Qǐng yòng (Fùshì) xiàngzhǐ.
When can I pick them up?	Shénme shíhou qǔ?
Can it be done earlier?	Néng zǎo yìdiǎn ma?
I'll be leaving town in (two) days.	(Liǎng) tiān hòu wǒ jiù zǒu le.

Returns and Repairs

I'd like to return this.	Wǒ xiǎng tuì huò.
It doesn't work.	Tā huài le.
Do you fix (cameras)?	Nǐmen xiū (zhàoxiàngjī) ma?
Something is wrong with the (shutter).	(Kuàimén) huài le.
Will you be able to fix it?	Néng xiū ma?
When will it be fixed?	Shénme shíhou néng xiū hǎo?

135的

100度的

我想要柯达胶卷。

哪儿能冲反转片？

我要冲胶卷。

不要扩印。

我想加印几张。

这个请印一张。

请用富士相纸。

什么时候取？

能早一点吗？

两天后我就走了。

我想退货。

它坏了。

你们修照相机吗？

快门坏了。

能修吗？

什么时候能修好？

V: *Xíng. Mài gěi nǐ suàn le.*
All right. I might as well sell it to you.

Renminbi

China's legal tender is Renminbi (RMB). Foreign currencies can not be used directly in China, though some shops illegally accept foreign currencies.

Foreign currencies may be converted into RMB at all banks, bank branches or in hotels, at the exchange rate quoted on the foreign exchange market on the day, minus a service charge.

Black market in foreign currency is forbidden in China. People may approach you in front of hotels, at tourist spots, or at banks for a black market exchange. You should be extremely careful. The exchange rate may be attractive—higher than the bank rate—but it is illegal and you risk being cheated.

What You'll Hear

bú mài	not for sale
Duōdà de?	How large?
huài le	broken
Jǐ hào de?	What size?
jiāoqián	pay
mài wánle	sold out
méi huò	out of stock
Nín yào shénme?	May I help you?
shōukuǎnchù	cashier's booth
yàngpǐn	sample
Zhǐ yǒu zhè yí gè.	It's the only one left.

Signs

bǎihuò shāngdiàn
Department Store

gōngyì měishù shāngdiàn
Arts and Crafts Store

dà jiǎnjià
Reduced Prices

shōu kuǎn tái
Cashier's Booth

yíngyè shíjiān
Business Hours

Entertainment

九
jiǔ **9**

Zài lái yí gè!
Encore!

While in China, you can enjoy various kinds of evening entertainment. Most cities will have a few cultural performances going on each night, with the major cities offering many. The possibilities range from theater to song and dance, acrobatics, traditional Chinese music, and local opera. Occasionally you might even luck in on a special event, such as a sports competition or circus. If you feel ambitious, there's always the local cinema.

ENTERTAINMENT

Choosing a Show

I'd like to see a (play).
Wǒ xiǎng kàn (huàjù).

I'm very interested in (local opera).
Wǒ duì (dìfāng xì) hěn gǎnxìngqù.

Is the (performer) famous in China?
Nèi wèi (yǎnyuán) zài Zhōngguó yǒumíng ma?

When does the (concert) begin?
(Yīnyuèhuì) shénme shíhou kāishǐ?

May I bring a (tape recorder)?
Wǒ néng dài (lùyīnjī) ma?

When will the (show) be over?
(Jiémù) shénme shíhou jiéshù?

May we leave at (intermission)?
Wǒmen néng zài (mùjiān xiūxi shí) líkāi ma?

What (movie) is showing today?
Jīntiān yǎn shénme (diànyǐng)?

Is it in English?
Shì Yīngwén duìbái ma?

Are there English subtitles?
Yǒu Yīngwén zìmù ma?

Buying Tickets

I'd like (two) tickets for [tomorrow].
Wǒ yào mǎi (liǎng) zhāng [míngtiān] de piào.

In the (front section), please.
Qǐng gěi wǒ (qiánpái) de.

Getting Seated

Excuse me, where are these seats?
Duìbuqǐ, wǒmen de zuòwèizài nǎr?

What are your seat numbers?
Nǐmen de zuòwèi hào shì duōshao?

I believe those are our seats.
Zhè shì wǒmen de zuòwèi.

Is anyone sitting there?
Nàr yǒu rén ma?

我想看话剧。

我对地方戏很感兴趣。

那位演员在中国有名吗？

音乐会什么时候开始？

我能带录音机吗？

节目什么时候结束？

我们能在幕间休息时离开吗？

今天演什么电影？

是英文对白吗？

有英文字幕吗？

我要买两张明天的票。

请给我前排的。

对不起，我们的座位在哪儿？

你们的座位号是多少？

这是我们的座位。

那儿有人吗？

Musical Instruments

China s musical instruments have a long history. Some of them, such as the sè and the shēng, date from at least the Warring States Period (475-221 BC). When you go to a concert of traditional Chinese music, you can look for these instruments.

笛子	dízi	8-stop bamboo flute
二胡	èrhú	2-stringed fiddle, with lower register
古琴	gǔqín	7-stringed zither
京胡	jīnghú	2-stringed fiddle, with higher register
琵琶	pípa	4-stringed lute
三弦	sānxián	3-stringed guitar
瑟	sè	25-stringed zither
笙	shēng	Chinese mouth organ
唢呐	suǒnà	Chinese cornet (woodwind)
箫	xiāo	vertical bamboo flute
洋琴	yángqín	dulcimer
月琴	yuèqín	4-stringed round mandolin
筝	zhēng	many-stringed zither

Chinese Operas

There are many local Chinese operas, each with its own colorful style of music, dance, and costume. The six major ones are described below.

Beijing Opera: Developed in the mid-nineteenth century when Beijing was the capital of the Qing Dynasty, this opera's lively repertoire includes many stories about political and military struggles.

Continued

83

There is someone here already.   Zhèr yǐjīng yǒu rén le.

Where can I get a (program)?   Nǎr yǒu (jiémùdān)?

Asking for Background

Who is (the director)?   (Dǎoyǎn) shì shuí?

Who plays (the Emperor)?   Shuí yǎn (huángdì)?

What is the name of this (song-and-dance troupe)?   Zhè shì něige (gēwǔtuán)?

(Where) was the film shot?   Zhè bù diànyǐng zài (nǎr) pāi de?

(When) does the story take place?   Zhè gùshi fāshēng zài (shénme shíjiān)?

What (region) is this dance from?   Zhè shì shénme (dìfāng) de wǔdǎo?

How old are those (acrobats)?   Zhèxiē (zájì yǎnyuán) duōdà le?

How long have they (trained)?   Tāmen (xùnliàn) le duōcháng shíjiān?

Which (team) is that?   Nà shì něige (duì)?

What's the score?   Bǐfēn shì duōshao?

Showing Appreciation

This (music) is great.   Zhè (yīnyuè) zhēn bàng!

Where can I get a (tape) of it?   Nǎr mài zhèige (lùyīndài)?

The (show) was outstanding.   Zhège (jiémù) hěn chūsè.

It's been a really (pleasant) evening.   Jīnwǎn guò de zhēn (yúkuài).

I enjoyed it very much.   Wǒ fēicháng xǐhuan.

这儿已经有人了。

哪儿有节目单?

导演是谁?

谁演皇帝?

这是哪个歌舞团?

这部电影在哪儿拍的?

这故事发生在什么时间?

这是什么地方的舞蹈?

这些杂技演员多大了?

他们训练了多长时间?

那是哪个队?

比分是多少?

这音乐真棒!

哪儿卖这个录音带?

这个节目很出色。

今晚过得真愉快。

我非常喜欢。

Pingju Opera: Popular in northeastern areas such as Beijing, Tianjin, and Hebei, this is a lively and easy-to-understand folk opera.

Henan Opera: The rustic tunes of this opera are popular in Henan, Shaanxi, Shanxi, Hebei, Shandong, and Anhui provinces.

Kunshan Opera: With clear singing and gentle gestures, this is one of the oldest traditional operas in China. It originated in the Kunshan area of Jiangsu Province.

Shaoxing Opera: The lyrical tunes of this opera originated from the folk songs of Shengxian County in Zhejiang Province.

Cantonese Opera: This opera has rich musical instrumentation and is popular in Guangdong, Guangxi, Taiwan, Hong Kong, and Macao.

What You'll Hear

guānzhòng	audience
Hǎo!	Bravo!
Hǎo qiú!	Good shot! (sports)
Jiāyóu!	Faster ! Go ! (sports)
nǚshìmén, xiānshēngmén	ladies and gentlemen
Qǐng suí wǒ lái.	Please follow me.
xiūxi (shí) fēnzhōng	(ten)-minute intermission
Yǎnchū dào cǐ jiéshù.	The performance is now over.
Yǎnchū xiànzài kāishǐ.	The performance shall now begin.
Zài lái yí gèr!	Encore!

Signs

shànglǒu
Upstairs

xiàlǒu
Downstairs

dānhào
Odd Numbers

shuānghào
Even Numbers

kèmǎn
Sold Out

Wǒ tóuténg.
I've got a headache.

Hopefully you will never have to use this chapter, but if you ever do feel under the weather, the best thing to do is to take care of the illness quickly. Large hotels usually have a clinic or doctor's office for just that purpose, or you can go to any hospital. Once there, you will first be asked your name, age, nationality, and cities recently visited. Then it will be time to describe your complaints. The doctor may only know a few medical terms in English, so bear in mind the phrases here.

Getting Help

I need to (see a dentist).	*Wǒ yào (kàn yá)*.
Where is the (clinic)?	*(Yīwùsuǒ) zài nǎr?*
Please take me to the (hospital).	*Qǐng dài wǒ qù (yīyuàn)*.
Could you call an ambulance for me right away?	*Nǐ néng tì wǒ mǎshàng jiào jiùhùchē ma?*
When does the (clinic) open?	*(Yīwùsuǒ) shénme shíhou kāimén?*
Do they understand English?	*Tāmen dǒng yīngwén ma?*
(Can you get me) a female doctor?	*(qǐng gěi wǒ) zhǎogè nǚ yīshēng, hǎo ma?*

Complaints

It hurts when I (talk).	*Yì (shuōhuà) jiù téng*.
It hurts here.	*Zhèr téng*.
I don't feel well.	*Wǒ juéde bù shūfu*.
I feel (faint).	*Wǒ (tóuyūn)*.
I have a cold.	*Wǒ gǎnmào le*.
My arm is broken.	*Wǒ de shǒubì duàn le*.
My back went out.	*Wǒ de yāo niǔ le*.
I'm allergic to (penicillin).	*Wǒ duì (qīngméisù) guòmǐn*.
I have (diabetes).	*Wǒ yǒu (tángniàobìng)*.
I have (a cardiac condition).	*Wǒ yǒu (xīnzàngbìng)*.
I'm pregnant.	*Wǒ huáiyùn le*.

Requests

Please take my (temperature).	*Qǐng tì wǒ liáng yíxià (tǐwēn)*.
I don't want a blood transfusion.	*Wǒ búyào shūxuě*.
Please give me some (medicine).	*Qǐng gěi wǒ diǎn (yào)*.
I need some (aspirin).	*Wǒ yào diǎn (āsīpǐlín)*.

Where Does It Hurt?

When telling the doctor where you have pain, the best method is to point to the afflicted area. You can also try using the Chinese words below.

我要看牙。

医务所在哪儿？

请带我去医院。

你能替我马上叫救护车吗？

医务所什么时候开门？

他们懂英文吗？

请给我找个女医生，好吗？

一说话就疼。

这儿疼。

我觉得不舒服。

我头晕。

我感冒了。

我的手臂断了。

我的腰扭了。

我对青霉素过敏。

我有糖尿病。

我有心脏病。

我怀孕了。

请替我量一下体温。

我不要输血。

请给我点药。

我要点阿斯匹林。

ankle: *jiǎowàn*	脚腕
back: *bèibù*	背部
bone: *gútou*	骨头
ear: *ěrduo*	耳朵
eye: *yǎnjīng*	眼睛
hand: *shǒu*	手
head: *tóu*	头
heart: *xīnzàng*	心脏
hip: *kuà*	胯
joint: *guānjié*	关节
knee: *xīgài*	膝盖
leg: *tuǐ*	腿
muscle: *jīròu*	肌肉
neck: *bózi*	脖子
shoulder: *jiānbǎng*	肩膀
stomach: *wèi*	胃
throat: *hóulóng*	喉咙
tooth: *yáchǐ*	牙齿

Doctor, I Have...

Many of the common ailments of China travelers are due to the change of environment plus the fatigue of being on the road. The doctor will prescribe either traditional herbal medicines (quite effective) or Western pharmaceuticals. Here's how to describe your symptoms:

I have
Wǒ 我...
a cold
gǎnmào le 感冒了

continued

| Will you fill this prescription, please? | Qǐng àn zhèzhāng chǔfāng pèi yào. |
| I need a (new) pair of glasses. | Wǒ xūyào yí fù (xīn) yǎnjìng. |

Questions

Is it (a contagious disease)?	Shì (chuánrǎnbìng) ma?
Can I (travel) tomorrow?	Míngtiān wǒ néng (qù lǚxíng) ma?
How long will this (illness) last?	Zhèige (bìng) shénmeshíhou néng hǎo?
How should this medicine be taken?	Zhèige yào zěnme chī fǎ?
Should I take all this medicine?	Zhèxiē yào dōu chī le ma?
Take one pill three times a day after meals.	Yìtiān sān cì, měicì yílì, fàn hòu fúyòng.
Do I need to come back for another session?	Wǒ hái yào zài lái kàn ma?

Taking Leave

You should have a thorough check-up.	Nǐ yīnggāi hǎohǎo de jiǎnchá yíxià.
I still feel rather weak.	Wǒ gǎnjué háihěn xūruò.
I feel much better now.	Wǒ gǎnjué hǎo duō le.
Thank you, doctor.	Xièxie nín, dàifu.

Dentist

Is there a good dentist here?	Zhèr yǒu hǎo de yáyī ma?
I have a toothache.	Wǒ yá téng.
I've lost a filling.	Wǒ de bǔyá tiánliào diào le.
I've broken a tooth.	Wǒ de yī kē yá duàn le.
I don't want it extracted.	Qǐng búyào bádiào.
Please give me an anaesthetic.	Qǐng gěi wǒ dǎ máyào.

请按这张处方配药。

我需要一副（新）眼镜。

是传染病吗？

明天我能去旅行吗？

这个病什么时候能好？

这个药怎么吃法？

这些药都吃了吗？

一天三次，每次一粒，饭后服用。

我还要再来看吗？

你应该好好地检查一下。

我感觉还很虚弱。

我感觉好多了。

谢谢您，大夫。

这有好的牙医吗？

我牙疼。

我的补牙填料掉了。

我的一颗牙断了。

请不要拔掉。

请给我打麻药。

constipation		
yǒu diǎn biànmì	有点便秘	
a cough		
yǒu diǎn késou	有点咳嗽	
diarrhea		
lā dùzi	拉肚子	
a fever		
fāshāo	发烧	
a headache		
tóuténg	头疼	
indigestion		
xiāohuà bù liáng	消化不良	
an infection		
fāyán le	发炎了	
insomnia		
shīmián	失眠	
nasal congestion		
bízi bù tōng qì	鼻子不通气	
a sore throat		
hóulóng tòng	喉咙痛	
a sprained ankle		
jiǎowàn niǔ le	脚腕扭了	

What You'll Hear

dǎzhēn	injection
jiā zài yèxià	put under your arm
liáng tǐwēn	take a temperature
měicì chī…	each time take...
Nǎli bù shūfu?	Where is the discomfort?
pào zài rèshuǐ lǐ	steep in hot water
tǎng xià	lie down
xiūxi	rest
yàofāng	prescription
yì tiān chī (sān) cì	take it (three) times a day

Signs

rénmín yīyuàn
People's Hospital

guàhào chù
Registration Office

ménzhěn bù
Outpatient Department

jízhěn shì
Emergency Room

yàofáng
Pharmacy

English-Chinese Dictionary

This is a simplified dictionary for the China traveler. The Chinese expressions here are colloquial equivalents, not academic translations, of the English entries. Where an entry has several meanings, a clarification of the intended meaning appears in parentheses. Abbreviations used are: noun (n), verb (v), and adjective (adj). Be aware that some Chinese expressions cannot be used syntactically like the corresponding English. However, they can be used effectively as replacements within the sentence patterns of the text.

a, an	yī, yígè	一，一个
a few	jǐgè	几个
a little	yìdiǎn	一点
a while	yìhuǐr	一会儿
abortion	liúchǎn	流产
about (approximately)	dàyuē	大约
about (concerning)	guānyú	关于
above	zài... zhī shàng	在……之上
accept	jiēshòu	接受
accident	shìgù, yìwài	事故，意外
accompaniment (music)	bànzòu	伴奏
accompany	péi	陪
accordion	shǒufēngqín	手风琴
accurate	zhèngquè, zhǔnquè	正确，准确
achievement	chéngjì, chéngguǒ	成绩，成果
acre	yīngmǔ	英亩
acrid	sè	涩
acrobat	zájì yǎnyuán	杂技演员
acrobatics	zájì	杂技
acrylic (fiber)	bǐnglún	丙纶
acting (performance)	biǎoyǎn	表演
action	xíngdòng, dòngzuò	行动，动作
activity	huódòng	活动
actor (actress)	yǎnyuán	演员
acupressure	diǎnxuè fǎ	点穴法
acupuncture	zhēnjiǔ	针灸

DICTIONARY

acupuncture anesthesia	*zhēncì mázuì*	针刺麻醉
acute	*jíxìng*	急性
adaptor (outlet board)	*jiēxiànbǎn*	接线板
adaptor (outlet cube)	*sāntōng*	三通
adaptor plug	*zhuǎnjiē chātóu*	转接插头
add	*jiā*	加
address (n)	*dìzhǐ*	地址
address book	*dìzhǐbù*	地址簿
addressee	*shōujiàn rén, duìfāng*	收件人，对方
adhesive plaster	*xiàngpí gāo*	橡皮膏
adjust	*tiáo*	调
adjustment	*tiáozhěng*	调整
administrator	*guǎnlǐ zhě*	管理者
adore	*rè ài*	热爱
adult	*chéngrén, dàrén*	成人，大人
advanced	*xiānjìn*	先进
advertisement manager	*guǎnggào jīnglǐ*	广告经理
aerobics	*jiànměi cāo*	健美操
affair (matter)	*shìqing*	事情
afraid	*pà*	怕
Africa	*Fēizhōu*	非洲
after meals	*fànhòu*	饭后
afternoon	*xiàwǔ*	下午
again	*zài*	再
agate	*mǎnǎo*	玛瑙
age (of a person)	*niánlíng*	年龄
agriculture	*nóngyè*	农业
AIDS	*àizī bìng*	艾滋病
air	*kōngqì*	空气
air conditioner	*kōngtiáojī*	空调机
air conditioning	*kōngtiáo*	空调
air force	*kōngjūn*	空军
air pump	*qìbèng, qìtǒng*	气泵，气筒
air sick	*yūnjī*	晕机
air valve	*qìfá, qìmén*	气阀，气门
airline	*hángkōng gōngsī*	航空公司
airmail	*hángkōng yóujiàn*	航空邮件
airplane	*fēijī*	飞机
airport	*fēijīchǎng*	飞机场
airport departure tax	*jīchǎng fèi*	机场费

aisle	*guòdào*	过道
alarm clock	*nàozhōng*	闹钟
alcohol (fluid)	*jiǔjīng*	酒精
alcohol (liquor)	*jiǔ*	酒
alike	*yíyàng, xiàng*	一样，像
all	*quánbù, dōu*	全部，都
allergic	*guòmǐn*	过敏
allergy	*guòmǐn zhèng*	过敏症
alley	*hútong*	胡同
almond	*xìngrén*	杏仁
almond-flour tea	*xìngrénchá*	杏仁茶
almond gelatin	*xìngrén dòufu*	杏仁豆腐
alone	*dāndú*	单独
already	*yǐjīng*	已经
also	*yě*	也
altitude	*hǎibá*	海拔
altogether	*yígòng*	一共
always	*zǒngshì, lǎoshì*	总是，老是
ambulance	*jiùhùchē*	救护车
analyze	*fēnxī*	分析
ancient	*gǔdài*	古代
and	*hé, gēn*	和，跟
anemia	*pínxuě zhèng*	贫血症
anesthesia	*mázuì*	麻醉
anesthetist	*mázuì shī*	麻醉师
angina pectoris	*xīn jiǎotòng*	心绞痛
angry	*shēngqì*	生气
animal	*dòngwù*	动物
ankle	*jiǎowàn*	脚腕
anniversary	*zhōunián*	周年
another	*lìng yí yè, biéde*	另一个，别的
answer (phone)	*jiē*	接
answer (reply)	*huídá*	回答
ant	*mǎyǐ*	蚂蚁
antenna	*tiānxiàn*	天线
(for TV, radio)		
anthropology	*rénlèixué*	人类学
antibiotic	*kàngshēngsù*	抗生素
antipyretic	*tuìshāo*	退烧
antique	*gǔdǒng*	古董
antiseptic cream	*xiāodú gāo*	消毒膏

DICTIONARY

anxious	zhāojí	着急
any	rènhé	任何
apartment	dānyuán fáng, gōngyù	单元房，公寓
appendix	lánwěi	阑尾
appetite	wèikǒu	胃口
applause	gǔzhǎng	鼓掌
apple	píngguǒ	苹果
apply for	shēnqǐng	申请
appreciate	xīnshǎng	欣赏
apprentice	xuétú	学徒
appropriate	héshì	合适
apricot	xìng	杏
April	sìyuè	四月
archaeology	kǎogǔ	考古
architecture	jiànzhù	建筑
area (measure)	miànjī	面积
area (realm)	lǐngyù, fànwéi	领域，范围
area (region)	dìqū	地区
argali sheep	tānyáng	滩羊
arm	gēbo, shǒubì	胳膊，手臂
armband	bìzhāng	臂章
armpit	yè	腋
army	bùduì, jūnduì	部队，军队
around (approximately)	zuǒyòu	左右
arrange	ānpái	安排
arrangement	ānpái	安排
arrive	dàodá	到达
art	yìshù	艺术
art director	yìshù zhǐdǎo	艺术指导
art exhibition	měishù zhǎnlǎn	美术展览
art gallery	huàláng	画廊
art museum	měishùguǎn	美术馆
art work	yìshùpǐn	艺术品
arthritis	guānjiéyán	关节炎
article (object)	wùpǐn	物品
artist	yìshùjiā	艺术家
arts and crafts	gōngyì měishù	工艺美术
arts and crafts store	gōngyì měishù shāngdiàn	工艺美术商店
ashtray	yānhuīgāng	烟灰缸
Asia	yàzhōu	亚洲
ask	wèn	问

asparagus lettuce	*wōsǔn*	莴笋
aspen tree	*báiyángshù*	白杨树
aspirin	*āsīpǐlín*	阿斯匹林
assistant (n)	*zhùshǒu, zhùlǐ*	助手，助理
assistant manager (hotel)	*dàtáng jīnglǐ*	大堂经理
assorted	*jīngxuǎn*	精选
assorted cold dishes	*lěng pīnpán*	冷拼盘
asthma	*xiàochuǎn*	哮喘
at	*zài*	在
athlete	*yùndòngyuán*	运动员
Atlantic Ocean	*Dàxīyáng*	大西洋
Atomic	*yuánzǐ*	原子
attend class	*shàngkè*	上课
attend school	*shàngxué*	上学
attention	*zhùyì*	注意
audience	*guānzhòng*	观众
auditorium	*lǐtáng*	礼堂
August	*bāyuè*	八月
aunt (see Appendix H)	*āyí*	阿姨
Australia	*àodàlìyà*	澳大利亚
Australian dollar	*àoyuán*	澳元
author	*zuòzhě*	作者
automatic	*zìdòng*	自动
autumn	*qiūtiān*	秋天
avenue	*dàjiē*	大街
awhile	*yìhuǐr*	一会儿
azalea	*dùjuānhuā*	杜鹃花
back (direction)	*hòu*	后
back (n)	*bèi*	背
back door	*hòumén*	后门
back section (seating)	*hòupái*	后排
backpack	*shuāngjiān bèibāo*	双肩背包
backstage	*hòutái*	后台
backyard	*hòuyuàn*	后院
bad	*huài*	坏
badminton	*yǔmáoqiú*	羽毛球
bag	*dài, dàizi*	袋，袋子
baggage	*xíngli*	行李
baggage cart	*xíngli chē*	行李车
baggage claim area	*xíngli tīng*	行李厅
baggage claim office	*xíngli bàngōng shì*	行李办公室

DICTIONARY

baggage strap	*xíngli dài*	行李带
baggage tag	*xíngli pái*	行李牌
balcony (seating)	*lóushàng zuòwei*	楼上座位
balcony (terrace)	*yángtái*	阳台
Bali	*bālí*	巴厘
ball	*qiú*	球
ball game	*qiúsài*	球赛
ballet	*bāléiwǔ*	芭蕾舞
ballpoint pen	*yuánzhūbǐ*	圆珠笔
ballroom	*wǔtīng*	舞厅
bamboo	*zhúzi*	竹子
bamboo shoot	*zhúsǔn*	竹笋
bambooware	*zhúbiān*	竹编
banana	*xiāngjiāo*	香蕉
band (music group)	*yuèduì*	乐队
band (radio)	*bōduàn*	波段
Band-Aid	*chuāngkětiē*	创可贴
bandage (n)	*bēngdài*	绷带
Bangkok	*màngǔ*	曼谷
bank (financial)	*yínháng*	银行
banquet	*yànhuì*	宴会
banquet manager	*yànhuìtīng jīnglǐ*	宴会厅经理
banyan tree	*róngshù*	榕树
bar (for drinks)	*jiǔbā*	酒吧
barbecue	*shāokǎo*	烧烤
barber shop	*lǐfà diàn*	理发店
bargain prices	*yìjià*	议价
barley	*dàmài. qīngkē*	大麦，青稞
baseball	*bàngqiú*	棒球
basin (land)	*péndì*	盆地
basketball	*lánqiú*	篮球
bat	*biānfú*	蝙蝠
bath towel	*yùjīn*	浴巾
bathhouse	*zǎotáng*	澡堂
bathroom (for baths)	*yùshì*	浴室
bathroom (toilet)	*cèsuǒ*	厕所
bathtub	*yùgāng*	浴缸
batik	*làrǎn*	蜡染
battery	*diànchí*	电池
bayberry, red	*yángméi*	杨梅
be	*shì*	是
beach	*hǎitān*	海滩

bean	*dòuzi*	豆子
bean paste	*dòushā*	豆沙
bean sauce, hot	*dòubàn jiàng*	豆瓣酱
bean sprout	*dòuyá*	豆芽
beancurd	*dòufu*	豆腐
bear (n)	*xióng. gǒuxióng*	熊，狗熊
beautiful	*měilì, piàoliang*	美丽，漂亮
beauty salon	*fàláng*	发廊
beaver	*hǎilí*	海狸
because	*yīnwéi*	因为
bed	*chuáng*	床
bedroom	*wòshì*	卧室
bedtime	*shuìjiào shíjiān*	睡觉时间
beef	*niúròu*	牛肉
beefsteak	*niúpái*	牛排
beer	*píjiǔ*	啤酒
beet	*tiáncài*	甜菜
before	*yǐqián*	以前
before meals	*fànqián*	饭前
before sleep	*shuìqián*	睡前
beggar	*qǐgài*	乞丐
begin	*kāishǐ*	开始
begonia	*qiūhǎitáng*	秋海棠
Beijing Opera	*jīngjù*	京剧
Belgium	*bǐlìshí*	比利时
believe (faith)	*xiāngxìn*	相信
believe (opinion)	*rènwéi*	认为
bell (ancient)	*gǔzhōng*	古钟
bell captain	*xíngli lǐngbān*	行李领班
bell tower	*zhōnglóu*	钟楼
belong to	*shǔyú*	属于
below	*zài...xiàmiàn*	在……下面
Berlin	*bólín*	柏林
berth	*chuángwèi*	床位
best	*zuìhǎo*	最好
better	*gènghǎo*	更好
bicycle	*zìxíngchē*	自行车
big	*dà*	大
bill (money notes)	*piàozi*	票子
bill (payment due)	*zhàngdān*	账单
billiards	*táiqiú*	台球
billion	*shíyì*	十亿

DICTIONARY

biology	shēngwùxué	生物学
bird	niǎo	鸟
birthday	shēngrì	生日
biscuit	bǐnggān	饼干
bite (v)	yǎo	咬
bitter	kǔ	苦
bitter gourd	kǔguā	苦瓜
black	hēi	黑
black mushroom	xiānggū, dōnggū	香菇，冬菇
black tea	hóngchá	红茶
black-and-white	hēibái	黑白
blackboard	hēibǎn	黑板
bladder	pángguāng	膀胱
bland	dàn	淡
blank tape	kòngbái dài	空白带
blanket (n)	tǎnzi	毯子
bleed	liúxuè	流血
blister	shuǐpào	水泡
blocked (stopped up)	dǔsè	堵塞
blonde	jīnfà	金发
blood	xuèyè	血液
blood pressure	xuèyā	血压
blood type	xuèxíng	血型
blouse	nǚ chènshān	女衬衫
blow dry	chuīgān	吹干
blow dryer	chuīfēngjī	吹风机
blue	lán	蓝
blunt (dull)	dùn	钝
board game	qísài	棋赛
boarding pass	dēngjī pái	登机牌
boat	chuan, zhōu	船，舟
boat ride	chéngchuán	乘船
body (human)	shēntǐ	身体
boil (v)	shāokāi, zhǔ	烧开，煮
boiled dumplings	shuǐjiǎo	水饺
boiled egg	zhǔ jīdàn	煮鸡蛋
boiled water	kāishuǐ	开水
bok choy	báicài	白菜
bon voyage	yílù shùnfēng	一路顺风
bone	gǔtou	骨头
Bonn	bō ēn	波恩
bonsai	pénjǐng	盆景

bonus	jiǎngjīn	奖金
bock (n)	shū	书
booking office	dìngpiào chù	订票处
bookkeeper	kuàijì	会计
bookstore	shūdiàn	书店
boring	kūzào	枯燥
borrow	jiè	借
Boston	bōshìdùn	波士顿
bottle (n)	píngzi	瓶子
bottle opener	pínggài qǐzi	瓶盖起子
bourgeois	zīchǎn jiējí	资产阶级
bowel movement	dàbiàn	大便
bowels	chángzi	肠子
bowl (n)	wǎn	碗
bowling	bǎolíng qiú	保龄球
bowling alley	bǎolíng qiúchǎng	保龄球场
box (carton)	hézi	盒子
box office	shòupiàocāhù	售票处
boxing	quánjī	拳击
boy	nánhái	男孩
boyfriend	nán péngyǒu	男朋友
bracelet	shǒuzhuó	手镯
brain	nǎozi	脑子
braised	gānshāo	干烧
brakes	zhá, shāchē	闸，刹车
brandy	báilándì	白兰地
brass instrument	tóngguǎn yuèqì	铜管乐器
Bravo!	hǎo	好!
bread	miànbāo	面包
breakdancing	pīlì wǔ	霹雳舞
breakfast	zǎofàn	早饭
breast	xiōngbù	胸部
breathe	hūxī	呼吸
brick	zhuāntou	砖头
brick tea	zhuānchá	砖茶
bridge (n)	qiáo	桥
bright	liàng, xiānyàn	亮，鲜艳
brightness	liàngdù	亮度
bring	dài, ná	带，拿
Britain	yīngguó	英国
broad bean	cándòu	蚕豆
broadband(computing)	kuāndài	宽带

DICTIONARY

broadcasting station	guǎngbō diàntái	广播电台
brocade	zhījín	织锦
broccoli	lùcàihuā	绿菜花
broken (out of order)	huài le	坏了
broken (severed)	duàn le	断了
bronchitis	zhī qìguǎn yán	支气管炎
bronze chariot	tóng zhànchē	铜战车
broom	tiáozhou	笤帚
broth	qīngtāng	清汤
brother (older)	gēge	哥哥
brother (younger)	dìdi	弟弟
brown	zōngsè	棕色
brown paper	niúpí zhǐ	牛皮纸
brown sauce (braised in)	hóngshāo	红烧
brush	shuāzi	刷子
Brussels	bùlǔsàiěr	布鲁塞尔
bubble gum	pàopaotáng	泡泡糖
bucket	tǒng	桶
buddha	fó	佛
Buddhism	fójiào	佛教
building (n)	lóufáng. jiànzhù	楼房，建筑
bull	gōngniú	公牛
Bund (Shanghai)	wàitān	外滩
bureau (organization)	jú	局
bureau director	júzhǎng	局长
burial grounds	mùdì	墓地
burn (n)	shāoshāng	烧伤
bus (n)	gōnggòngqìchē	公共汽车
bus driver	gōnggòngqìchē sījī	公共汽车司机
bus map	gōnggòngqìchē xiànlù tú	公共汽车线路图
bus station	gōnggòngqìchē zǒngzhàn	公共汽车总站
bus stop	gōnggòngqìchē zhàn	公共汽车站
bushel	pǔshì ěr	蒲式耳
business	shēngyì	生意
business management	qǐyè guǎnlǐ	企业管理
business person	shāngrén	商人
busy	máng	忙
busy line (phone)	zhànxiàn	占线
but	dànshì	但是
butcher shop	ròudiàn	肉店
butter	huángyóu	黄油

buttocks	pìgu	屁股
button (for clothing)	kòuzi	扣子
button (pushbutton)	ànniǔ	按钮
buy	mǎi	买
CAAC	zhōngguó mínháng	中国民航
cabbage	yáng báicài	洋白菜
cabbage heart	càixīn	菜心
cabbage, Chinese	dà báicài	大白菜
cabin (ship)	cāng, chuáncāng	舱，船舱
cable address	diànbào guàhào	电报挂号
cable TV	yǒuxiàn diànshì	有线电视
cadre	gànbù	干部
cadre's jacket	zhōngshān zhuāng	中山装
cafe	kāfēiguǎn	咖啡馆
cake	dàngāo	蛋糕
calendar	rìlì	日历
California	jiāzhōu	加州
call (to beckon)	jiào	叫
call (to telephone)	gěi…dǎdiànhuà	给……打电话
calligrapher	shūfǎjiā	书法家
calligraphy	shūfǎ	书法
calligraphy brush	máobǐ	毛笔
camel	luòtuo	骆驼
camellia	cháhuā	茶花
camera	zhàoxiàngjī	照相机
camp, camping	lùyíng	露营
camphor tree	zhāngshù	樟树
can (know how to)	huì	会
can (possible to)	néng	能
can (tin, jar)	guàntou	罐头
can opener	guàntou qǐzi	罐头起子
Canada	jiānádà	加拿大
canal	yùnhé	运河
cancel	qǔxiāo	取消
cancer	áizhèng	癌症
candied haws	bīngtáng húlu	冰糖葫芦
candle	làzhú	蜡烛
candy	táng, tángguǒ	糖，糖果
canoe	dúmùzhōu	独木舟
Canon	jiānéng	佳能
Cantonese Opera	yuèjù	粤剧
capital (city)	shǒudū	首都

DICTIONARY

capital (money)	zījīn, zīběn	资金，资本
capitalist (n)	zīběnjiā	资本家
capon	yānjī	阉鸡
Cappuccino	kǎbùqínuò	卡布奇诺
capsule	jiāonáng	胶囊
caption	zìmù	字幕
car	qìchē, xiǎojiàochē	汽车，小轿车
car sick	yùnchē	晕车
cardiac failure	xīnlì shuāijié	心力衰竭
cardiology	xīnzàng bìngxué	心脏病学
cards (playing)	púkè pái	扑克牌
career	shìyè	事业
careful	xiǎoxīn	小心
careless	mǎdàhā	马大哈
carpenter	mùjiàng	木匠
carpet	dìtǎn	地毯
carrot	húluóbo	胡萝卜
carry	xiédài	携带
carry-on luggage	shǒutí xíngli	手提行李
cart (n)	tuīchē	推车
cartoon (film)	dònghuà piān	动画片
cartoon (print)	mànhuà	漫画
carving (n)	diāokè	雕刻
cash (n)	xiànjīn	现金
cash (v)	duìhuàn	兑换
cash advance	xiànjīn yùfù	现金预付
cashew nut	yāoguǒ	腰果
cashier	chūnàyuán	出纳员
cashier's booth	shōukuǎnchù	收款处
cashmere	kāishìmǐ	开士米
casserole	shāguō	沙锅
cassette (sound tape)	cídài	磁带
cassia	guìhuā	桂花
cassia wine	guìhuājiǔ	桂花酒
casual	suíbiàn	随便
cat	māo	猫
catch (v)	zhuāzhù	抓住
cathartic	xièyào	泻药
cattle	shēngkou	牲口
cauliflower	càihuā	菜花
cave	shāndòng	山洞
CCTV	zhōngyāng diànshìtái	中央电视台
English Service	yīngyǔ jiémù	英语节目

CD	*guāngpán*	光盘
ceiling	*tiānhuābǎn*	天花板
celery	*qíncài*	芹菜
cellophane tape	*tòumíng jiāodài*	透明胶带
cell phone	*shǒujī*	手机
cement (concrete)	*shuǐní*	水泥
center (middle)	*zhōngjiān*	中间
centigrade	*shèshì*	摄氏
centimeter	*límǐ*	厘米
Central America	*zhōngměizhōu*	中美洲
century	*shìjì*	世纪
ceramics	*táocí*	陶瓷
certain	*yídìng*	一定
certificate	*zhèngmíng*	证明
chain	*liàntiáo, liànzi*	链条，链子
chair (n)	*yǐzi*	椅子
chairman	*zhǔxí*	主席
Chairman Mao	*máo zhǔxí*	毛主席
chamber music	*shìnèi yuè*	室内乐
champagne	*xiāngbīnjiǔ*	香槟酒
champion	*guànjūn*	冠军
chance (opportunity)	*jīhuì*	机会
change	*língqián*	零钱
(coins, small bills)		
change	*huàn*	换
(to replace, exchange)		
change (transfer)	*diào*	调
change	*biàndào*	变化
(transformation)		
channel (TV)	*píndào*	频道
character (role)	*juésè*	角色
characteristic	*tèdiǎn*	特点
charcoal drawing	*tànhuà*	炭画
charge d'affaires	*dàibàn*	代办
charming	*mírén*	迷人
cheap	*piányi*	便宜
cheapest	*zuìpiányi*	最便宜
check, bank	*zhīpiào*	支票
check in (for flight)	*bàn chéngjī shǒuxù*	办乘机手续
check in (register)	*dēngjì*	登记
check out	*tuìfáng*	退房
(from a hotel)		
checkers, Chinese	*tiàoqí*	跳棋

DICTIONARY

Cheers!	gānbēi	干杯!
cheese	nǎilào	奶酪
chef	chúshī	厨师
chemical (adj)	huàxué de	化学的
chemist's (drugstore)	yàodiàn	药店
chemistry	huàxué	化学
chemotherapy	huàliáo	化疗
cheongsam (gown)	qípáo	旗袍
cherry	yīngtáo	樱桃
chess	guójì xiàngqí	国际象棋
chess, Chinese	xiàngqí	象棋
chest	xiōngqiāng	胸腔
chest pain	xiōngkǒu tòng	胸口痛
chestnut	lìzi	栗子
chewing gum	kǒuxiāngtáng	口香糖
Chicago	zhījiāgē	芝加哥
chicken	jī	鸡
child	xiǎohái	小孩
children's clothing	tóngzhuāng	童装
children's palace	shàonián gōng	少年宫
chilli pepper (dried)	gān làjiāo	干辣椒
China	zhōngguó	中国
China Central Television (CCTV)	zhōngyāng diànshì tái	中央电视台
Chinese (language)	hànyǔ	汉语
Chinese character	hànzì	汉字
Chinese meal	zhōngcān	中餐
Chinese menu	zhōngcān càipǔ	中餐菜谱
Chinese New Year	chūnjié	春节
chives, Chinese	jiǔcài	韭菜
chocolate	qiǎokèlì	巧克力
choice	xuǎnzé	选择
cholera	huòluàn	霍乱
choose	xuǎn, tiāo	选，挑
chop (seal)	yìnzhāng shí, túzhāng	印章石，图章
chopsticks	kuàizi	筷子
chorus	héchàng	合唱
Christmas	shèngdànjié	圣诞节
chronic	mànxìng	慢性
chrysanthemum	júhuā	菊花
church	jiàotáng	教堂
cigarette	xiāngyān	香烟

cinema	diànyǐng yuàn	电影院
circle (n)	quān	圈
circus	mǎxì	马戏
citizen	gōngmín	公民
city	chéngshì	城市
city gate	chéngmén	城门
city map	chéngshì jiāotōng tú	城市交通图
city tour	yóulǎn shìróng	游览市容
civil	mínyòng	民用
clams	géli	蛤蜊
clap (applaud)	gǔzhǎng	鼓掌
class (social)	jiējí	阶级
class (students)	bān	班
classic	gǔdiǎn	古典
classroom	jiàoshì, kètáng	教室，课堂
clay	niántǔ	粘土
clay figure	nírén	泥人
clean (adj)	gānjìng	干净
clean (v)	dǎsǎo	打扫
cleaning solution	xiāodú yè	消毒液
clear (distinct)	qīngchǔ	清楚
cliff	xuányá	悬崖
climb	pá	爬
clinic	wèishēngsuǒ	卫生所
clock	zhōng	钟
cloisonne	jǐngtàilán	景泰蓝
cloisonne vase	jǐngtàilán huāpíng	景泰蓝花瓶
close (to shut)	guān	关
closed (business)	guānmén	关门
closed (not public)	bù kāifàng	不开放
closet	yīguì	衣柜
cloth	bù, liàozi	布，料子
clothes hanger	yījià	衣架
clothespin	yīfujiā	衣服夹
clothing	yīfu	衣服
clothing store	fúzhuāng diàn	服装店
cloud	yún	云
cloudy weather	yīn, duōyún	阴，多云
club (recreation)	jùlèbù	俱乐部
coach (sports)	jiàoliàn	教练
coal	méi	煤
coat	shàngyī, dàyī	上衣，大衣

DICTIONARY

coat hanger	yījià	衣架
Coca-Cola	kěkǒu kělè	可口可乐
cocaine	kěkǎyīn	可卡因
cock's comb (flower)	jīguānhuā	鸡冠花
cockroach	zhāngláng	蟑螂
cocoa	kěkě	可可
coconut	yēzi	椰子
cocoon	cánjiǎn	蚕茧
coffee	kāfēi	咖啡
coffee shop	kāfēi diàn	咖啡店
cola	kělè	可乐
cold (adj)	lěng	冷
cold (illness)	gǎnmào, zhāoliáng	感冒，着凉
cold drink	lěngyǐn	冷饮
cold drinking water	liángbáikāi	凉白开
cold milk	lěng niúnǎi	冷牛奶
cold platter	lěngpán	冷盘
cold water (from tap)	lěngshuǐ	冷水
cold-water wash	lěngshuǐ xǐ	冷水洗
cold wave (perm)	lěngtàng	冷烫
collect (gather)	shōují	收集
collect (phone call)	duìfāng fùkuǎn	对方付款
college	xuéyuàn, dàxué	学院，大学
color (n)	yánsè	颜色
color TV	cǎidiàn	彩电
colored	cǎisè	彩色
column (pillar)	zhùzi	柱子
coma	hūnmí	昏迷
comb (n)	shūzi	梳子
come	lái	来
comedy	xǐjù	喜剧
comfortable	shūfu	舒服
commemorative stamp	jìniàn yóupiào	纪念邮票
common	pǔtōng	普通
commune	gōngshè	公社
communist party	gòngchǎndǎng	共产党
compact disc	jīguāng chàngpiàn	激光唱片
company (business)	gōngsī	公司
company account	gōngsī zhànghù	公司帐户
compass	zhǐnánzhēn	指南针
complain	bàoyuàn	抱怨

completely	wánquán	完全
composer (music)	zuòqǔjiā	作曲家
composition (music)	zuòpǐn	作品
composition (painting)	gòutú	构图
comprehensive	zōnghé	综合
computer	jìsuànjī, diànnǎo	计算机，电脑
computer programmer	diànnǎo chéngxùyuán	电脑程序员
comrade	tóngzhì	同志
concerning	guānyú	关于
concert	yīnyuèhuì	音乐会
concert hall	yīnyuè tīng	音乐厅
concierge (hotel)	jiēdàiyuán	接待员
concubine	fēizi, qiè	妃子，姜
condition	tiáojiàn, qíngkuàng	条件，情况
conditioner (for hair)	hùfàsù	护发素
condom	bìyùn tào	避孕套
conductor (bus)	shòupiàoyuán	售票员
conductor (music)	zhǐhuī	指挥
conductor (train)	chéngwùyuán	乘务员
conference room	huìyìshì	会议室
confirm	quèdìng	确定
connect	jiē	接
connecting flight	xiánjiē hángbān	衔接航班
connection (relation)	guānxi	关系
conscience	liángxīn	良心
consider	kǎolù	考虑
consomme	qīngtāng	清汤
constipation	biànmì	便秘
Constitution	xiànfǎ	宪法
construction	jiànshè	建设
contact lens	yǐnxíng yǎnjìng	隐形眼镜
contact prints (photo)	xiǎoyàng	小样
contagious	jiēchù chuánrǎn	接触传染
container	róngqì	容器
contemporary (adj)	dāngdài	当代
continent	dàlù	大陆
contraceptives	bìyùn yòngpǐn	避孕用品
contrast (n)	duìbǐ	对比
convenient	fāngbiàn	方便
convulsion	jīngluán	痉挛
cook (n)	chúshī, dà shīfu	厨师，大师傅

DICTIONARY

cook (prepare meals)	*zuòfàn*	做饭
cookie	*bǐnggān*	饼干
cooking	*pēngtiáo*	烹调
cool (adj)	*liáng, liángkuài*	凉，凉快
copy (n)	*fùběn*	副本
corduroy	*dēngxīn róng*	灯芯绒
coriander	*xiāngcài*	香菜
cork carving	*ruǎnmù diāo*	软木雕
corkscrew	*píngsāi qǐzi*	瓶塞起子
corn	*yùmǐ*	玉米
cornet, Chinese	*suǒnà*	锁呐
corporation	*gōngsī*	公司
correct (yes)	*duì*	对
costume	*xìzhuāng*	戏装
cot	*zhédié chuáng*	折叠床
cottage (thatched)	*cǎofáng*	草房
cotton	*mián*	棉
cotton-padded jacket	*miányī*	棉衣
cotton-padded shoes	*miánxié*	棉鞋
cough	*késòu*	咳嗽
cough drops	*hánpiàn*	含片
cough syrup	*zhǐké tángjiāng*	止咳糖浆
country (nation)	*guójiā*	国家
country (rural)	*xiāngcūn*	乡村
country music	*xiāngcūn yīnyuè*	乡村音乐
country person	*xiāngxiàrén*	乡下人
countryside	*nóngcūn*	农村
county	*xiàn*	县
courtyard	*yuànzi*	院子
cover (n)	*gàizi*	盖子
cow	*nǎiniú*	奶牛
crab	*pángxiè*	螃蟹
crabapple, Chinese	*hǎitáng*	海棠
craft	*gōngyì*	工艺
craftsman	*gōngjiàng*	工匠
cramp	*chōujīn*	抽筋
crane	*hè*	鹤
crayon	*làbǐ*	蜡笔
cream (dairy)	*nǎiyóu*	奶油
creator	*chuàngzàozhě*	创造者
credit card	*xìnyòngkǎ*	信用卡
crepe (pancake)	*jiānbǐng*	煎饼

crispy	cuì	脆
crispy duck	xiāngsū yā	香酥鸭
critical condition	qíngkuàng wēijí	情况危急
crop (n)	nóngzuòwù	农作物
cross (pass)	guò	过
cross talk	xiàngsheng	相声
(comedy routine)		
crosswalk	rénxíng héngdào	人行横道
cruise (v)	yóu	游
cruise boat	yóutǐng	游艇
cry (sob)	kū	哭
cub	yòuzǎi	幼仔
cucumber	huángguā	黄瓜
cultural exchange	wénhuà jiāoliú	文化交流
cultural relic	wénhuà gǔjì	文化古迹
Cultural Revolution	wéngé	文革
culture	wénhuà	文化
(arts, customs)		
cup	bēi. bēizi	杯，杯子
curler (for hair)	fàjuǎn	发卷
curling iron	měifà qì	美发器
curly	juǎnqūde	卷曲的
curry	gālí	咖喱
curtain (theater)	mù	幕
curtain (window)	chuānglián	窗帘
cushion	diànzi	垫子
custom (tradition)	fēngsú	风俗
custom-made	dìngzuò de	定做的
customer	gùkè	顾客
customs	hǎiguān	海关
(at the border)		
customs declaration	hǎiguān shēnbào dān	海关申报单
customs duty	guānshuì	关税
cut (v)	jiǎn. qiē	剪，切
cuttlefish	mòdǒuyú, wūzéi	墨斗鱼，乌贼
cycling	qí zìxíngchē	骑自行车
cymbals	chǎ	镲
cypress tree	bǎishù	柏树
cystitis	pángguāngyán	膀胱炎
daily (newspaper)	rìbào	日报
Dalai Lama	dálài lǎma	达赖喇嘛

DICTIONARY

dam	dībà	堤坝
damaged	nònghuài le	弄坏了
damp	shī	湿
dance (n)	wǔdǎo	舞蹈
dance (v)	tiàowǔ	跳舞
dance drama	wǔjù	舞剧
dance hall	wǔtīng	舞厅
dance party	wǔhuì	舞会
dance troupe	wǔdǎo tuán	舞蹈团
dancer	wǔdǎo yǎnyuán	舞蹈演员
danger	wēixiǎn	危险
dark	hēi	黑
darkroom	ànshì	暗室
date (appointment)	yuēhuì	约会
date (fruit)	zǎo	枣
dating (courtship)	tán liàn ài	谈恋爱
daughter	nǚér	女儿
day	rì, tiān	日，天
day after tomorrow	hòutiān	后天
day-lily bud	jīnzhēn	金针
daytime	báitiān	白天
deaf	lóng	聋
December	shí èryuè	十二月
decide	juédìng	决定
declare (at customs)	shēnbào	申报
decongestant	bítōng	鼻通
decoration	zhuāngshì	装饰
deep	shēn	深
deep-fried	zhá	炸
deer	lù	鹿
degree (temperature)	dù	度
delicatessen	shúshí diàn	熟食店
delicious	hǎochī	好吃
democracy	mínzhǔ	民主
demonstration (in street)	yóuxíng	游行
Denmark	dānmài	丹麦
dental floss	yáxiàn	牙线
dentist	yákē yīshēng	牙科医生
dentist's office	yákē zhěnsuǒ	牙科诊所
deodorant	chúchòujì	除臭剂
depart	líkāi	离开

department	bùmén, kē	部门，科
department store	bǎihuò shāngdiàn	百货商店
departure time (planes)	qǐfēi shíjiān	起飞时间
deposit (bank)	chǔxù	储蓄
deposit (pledge, security)	yājīn	押金
depressed (mood)	qíngxù bù hǎo	情绪不好
dermatologist	pífūkē yīshēng	皮肤科医生
dermatology department	pífūkē	皮肤科
descend	xià	下
descend (planes)	jiàngluò	降落
describe	xíngróng	形容
desert	shāmò	沙漠
design (v)	shèjì	设计
designer	shèjìshī	设计师
designer (name brand)	míngpái	名牌
desk	shūzhuō	书桌
dessert	diǎnxin	点心
detergent	qùwūfěn	去污粉
detour	wānlù	弯路
develop (film)	chōng, chōngxǐ	冲，冲洗
diabetes	tángniàobìng	糖尿病
diagnosis	zhěnduàn	诊断
dial (v)	bō	拨
dialog (theater)	duìbái	对白
diamond	zuànshí	钻石
diaphragm (camera)	guāngquān	光圈
diarrhea	lā dùzi	拉肚子
diced meat or vegetable	dīng	丁
dictionary	zìdiǎn	字典
die (v)	sǐ, qùshì	死，去世
diet (foods eaten)	yǐnshí	饮食
diet (weight loss)	jiéshí	节食
dietician	yíngyǎng yīshī	营养医师
different	bù yíyàng	不一样
difficulty	kùnnán	困难
dig	wā	挖
digital camera	shùmǎ xiàngjī	数码相机
dignified	yǒu qìpài	有气派

DICTIONARY

diligent	qínfèn	勤奋
dim sum	diǎnxin	点心
dining car	cānchē	餐车
dining room	cāntīng	餐厅
dinner (supper)	wǎnfàn	晚饭
dip (v)	zhàn	蘸
diplomat	wàijiāoguān	外交官
diplomatic	wàijiāo	外交
director (artistic)	dǎoyǎn	导演
director	zhǔrèn	主任
(of an organization)		
dirty	zāng	脏
disabled person	cánjí rén	残疾人
disastrous	zāogāo	糟糕
disco	dísīkē	迪斯科
discomfort	bù shūfu	不舒服
discount (n)	zhékòu	折扣
discover	fāxiàn	发现
discussion	tǎolùn	讨论
dish (plate, tray)	pán	盘
dishwashing liquid	xǐdíjì	洗涤剂
disinfectant	xiāodú jì	消毒剂
disk film	pán shì jiāopiàn	盘式胶片
dislocated (joint)	tuōjiùle	脱白了
disperse	sàn	散
distance	jùlí	距离
district	qū	区
disturb	dǎrǎo, gānrǎo	打扰，干扰
divide	fēn	分
divorce	líhūn	离婚
dizzy	tóuyūn	头晕
do (be occupied with)	zuò	做
do business	zuò shēngyì	做生意
do not...	bié, búyào	别,不要……
dock (n)	mǎtóu	码头
doctor	yīshēng, dàifu	医生,大夫
documentary (film)	jìlù piān	纪录片
doesn't work	bù xíng	不行
dog	gǒu	狗
dollar	yuán	元
domestic (national)	guónèi	国内
don't mind (object to)	bú zàihu	不在乎

Donald Duck	tánglǎoyā	唐老鸭
door	mén	门
door god	ménshén	门神
dormitory	sùshè	宿舍
double (adj)	shuāng	双
double bed	shuāngrén chuáng	双人床
double happiness	shuāngxǐ	喜喜
double-sided embroidery	shuāngmiàn xiù	双面锈
dough figure	miànrén	面人
down	xià	下
downhill	xiàshān	下山
downstairs	lóuxià	楼下
downtown	shìzhōngxīn	市中心
dragon	lóng	龙
Dragon Well tea	lóngjǐng chá	龙井茶
dragon dance	lóngwǔ	龙舞
drain (n)	xiàshuǐdào	下水道
drama	xìjù	戏剧
drawing	túhuà	图画
drawing paper	túhuàzhǐ	图画纸
dress rehearsal	cǎipái	彩排
dresser	yīchú	衣橱
dressing room	huàzhuāng shì	化装室
dried beancurd	dòufu gān	豆腐干
dried shrimps	hǎimǐ	海米
drink	hē	喝
drive (v)	kāichē	开车
driver (bus, taxi)	sījī	司机
driver's license	jiàshǐ zhízhào	驾驶执照
drop (n)	dī	滴
drop (v)	diào	掉
drug	yào	药
drug (narcotic)	dúpǐn	毒品
drugstore	yàodiàn	药店
drum (n)	gǔ	鼓
drum tower	gǔlóu	鼓楼
dry	gān	干
dry clean	gānxǐ	干洗
dry white wine	gān bái pútao jiǔ	干白葡萄酒
dubbed film	yìzhì piān	译制片
duck	yāzi	鸭子

DICTIONARY

duet (instrumental)	*èrchóngzòu*	二重奏
duet (vocal)	*èrchóngchàng*	二重唱
dulcimer	*yángqín*	扬琴
dull (uninteresting)	*dāndiào, méi yìsi*	单调, 没意思
dumb (mute)	*yǎ*	哑
dumplings	*jiǎozi, bāozi*	饺子,包子
duplication machine	*fùyìn jī*	复印机
during	*zài...zhōng*	在……中
dustpan	*bòji*	簸箕
dusty	*huīchén duō*	灰尘多
dynasty	*cháodài*	朝代
dysentery	*lìji*	痢疾
each	*měi, měigè*	每, 每个
each time	*měicì*	每次
ear	*ěrduo*	耳朵
ear-nose-throat specialist	*ěrbíhóu kē dàifu*	耳鼻喉科大夫
early	*zǎo*	早
earn	*zhèng*	挣
earth (planet)	*dìqiú*	地球
earthquake	*dìzhèn*	地震
east	*dōng*	东
East China Sea	*dōnghǎi*	东海
easy	*róngyì*	容易
eat	*chī*	吃
Economic Daily	*jīngjì rìbào*	《经济日报》
economics	*jīngjìxué*	经济学
economy	*jīngjì*	经济
economy class	*pǔtōng cāngwèi*	普通舱位
edge	*biān*	边
editor	*biānjì*	编辑
education	*jiàoyù*	教育
eel	*shànyú*	鳝鱼
effect	*xiàoguǒ*	效果
efficiency	*xiàolǜ*	效率
egg	*jīdàn*	鸡蛋
egg-drop soup	*dànhuātāng*	蛋花汤
egg white	*dànbái, dànqīng*	蛋白, 蛋清
eggplant	*qiézi*	茄子
Egypt	*āijí*	埃及
eight	*bā*	八

eight precious rice	bābǎofàn	八宝饭
eighty	bāshí	八十
ejaculation	shèjīng	射精
elbow	zhǒu	肘
election	xuǎnjǔ	选举
electrical equipment	diànqì	电器
electricity	diàn	电
electronic	diànzǐ	电子
electrotherapy	diànliáo	电疗
elephant	dàxiàng	大象
elevator	diàntī	电梯
elm tree	yúshù	榆树
embarrassed	bùhǎo yìsi	不好意思
embassy	dàshǐguǎn	大使馆
embroidery	cìxiù	刺绣
emergency	jínjí qíngkuàng	紧急情况
emergency room	jízhěn shì	急诊室
emetic	cuītùjì	催吐剂
emperor	huángdì	皇帝
employee	gùyuán	雇员
empress	huánghòu, nǚhuáng	皇后,女皇
empress dowager	tàihòu	太后
empty (adj)	kōng	空
enamel	tángcí	搪瓷
encephalitis	nǎoyán	脑炎
encore	zài lái yí gè	再来一个
end (v)	jiéshù	结束
energy (spirit)	jīnglì	精力
engine	fādòngjī	发动机
engineer	gōngchéngshī	工程师
England	yīngguó	英国
English (language)	yīngyǔ	英语
engraving	diāokè	雕刻
enjoy	xǐhuan	喜欢
enlargement	fàngdà	放大
enough	zúgòu	足够
ensemble (instrumental)	hézòu	合奏
enter	jìn	进
entrance	rùkǒu, jìnkǒu	入口,进口
entrepreneur	qǐyè jiā	企业家
entry visa	rùjìng qiānzhèng	入境签证

DICTIONARY

envelope	*xìnfēng*	信封
epilepsy	*diānxián*	癫痫
episode	*chāqǔ*	插曲
equal (adj)	*píngděng, yíyàng*	平等, 一样
equal (v)	*děngyú*	等于
eraser	*xiàngpí*	橡皮
escalator	*zìdòng fútī*	自动扶梯
especially	*tèbié*	特别
espresso	*yìshì nóngkāfēi*	意式浓咖啡
et cetera	*děng*	等
ethnic minorities	*shǎoshù mínzú*	少数民族
eunuch	*tàijiān*	太监
Europe	*ōuzhōu*	欧洲
even (more)	*gèng*	更
evening	*wǎnshang*	晚上
everyday	*měitiān*	每天
everyone	*dàjiā*	大家
everything	*yíqiè*	一切
everywhere	*dàochù*	到处
evil	*huài*	坏
example	*lìzi*	例子
exceed	*chāoguò*	超过
excellent	*fēicháng hǎo*	非常好
excellent (slang)	*bàng*	棒
exchange (ideas)	*jiāoliú*	交流
exchange (money)	*duìhuàn*	兑换
exchange rate	*duìhuàn lù*	兑换率
exciting	*lìngrén jīdòng*	令人激动
excuse me (make way)	*láojia*	劳驾
excuse me (pardon)	*duìbuqǐ*	对不起
exercise (physical)	*duànliàn*	锻炼
exhibition	*zhǎnlǎn*	展览
exit (n)	*chūkǒu*	出口
exit visa	*chūjìng qiānzhèng*	出境签证
expectation	*qīwàng*	期望
expense	*fèiyòng*	费用
expensive	*guì*	贵
experience (n)	*jīngyàn*	经验
experiment	*shìyàn*	试验
expert	*zhuānjiā*	专家
expertise	*zhuāncháng*	专长

explain	jiěshì	解释
expert goods	chūkǒu huò	出口货
expert license	chūkǒu xǔkě zhèng	出口许可证
express (speed)	tèkuài	特快
express (to convey)	bǐaodá	表达
extension (phone)	fēnjī	分机
extension cord	diànxiàn	电线
external use	wàiyòng	外用
extra (surplus)	fùyù de	富余的
extra large	tèdà hào	特大号
extra small	tèxiǎo hào	特小号
extract a tooth	báyá	拔牙
extremely	jí	极
eye (n)	yǎnjing	眼睛
eye drops	yǎn yàoshuǐ	眼药水
face (n)	liǎn	脸
face cream	miànshuāng	面霜
facial (n)	měiróng	美容
factory	gōngchǎng	工厂
Fahrenheit	huáshì	华氏
faint	tóuyūn	头晕
fake	màopái	冒牌
fall (v)	shuāidǎo, diào	摔倒, 掉
false	jiǎ de	假的
family	jiā, jiātíng	家, 家庭
family members	iāntíng chéngyuán	家庭成员
fan, electric	diànshàn	电扇
fan, folding	zhéshàn	折扇
fan, hand-held	shànzi	扇子
Fantastic!	juéle	绝了!
far	yuǎn	远
fare	chēfèi	车费
(bus, taxi, or train)		
farm	nóngchǎng	农场
farmer	nóngmín	农民
farmer's home	nóngjiā	农家
fast (speed)	kuài	快
fast food	kuàicān	快餐
fat (adj)	pàng	胖
fat (n)	zhīfáng	脂肪
father	fùqin	父亲

DICTIONARY

faucet	lóngtóu	龙头
feature film	gùshì piān	故事片
February	èryuè	二月
fee	fèi	费
feel (sense)	juéde	觉得
female (animals)	cí, mǔ	雌, 母
female (people)	nǚ	女
fencing	jījiàn	击剑
fertilizer	féiliào	肥料
fever	fāshāo	发烧
few	hěnshǎo, bù duō	很少, 不多
fiction	xiǎoshuō	小说
fiddle, Beijing Opera	jīnghú	京胡
fiddle, two-stringed	èrhú	二胡
field (farm)	tián	田
field (for athletics)	yùndòng chǎng	运动场
fifty	wǔshí	五十
fig	wúhuāguǒ	无花果
fill a tooth	bǔyá	补牙
fill in (a form)	tián	填
film (for camera)	jiāojuǎn	胶卷
film (movie)	diànyǐng	电影
film festival	diànyǐng jié	电影节
film studio	diànyǐng chǎng	电影厂
final (adj)	zuìhòu	最后
finally	zhōngyú	终于
find (v)	zhǎo	找
fine (delicate)	jīngzhì	精致
fine (good)	hěnhǎo, tǐnghǎo	很好, 挺好
fine arts	měishù	美术
finger	shǒuzhǐ	手指
fingernail polish	zhījia yóu	指甲油
fingernail polish remover	xǐjiǎshuǐ	洗甲水
finish (v)	wánchéng	完成
finished	wán le	完了
Finland	fēnlán	芬兰
fire (n)	huǒ	火
fire equipment	mièhuǒ qì	灭火器
fire escape	ānquán tī	安全梯
fire exit	tàipíng mén	太平门
fire fighter	xiāofáng duìyuán	消防队员

first (beforehand)	xiān	先
first, the	dìyī	第一
first-aid kit	jíjiù yàoxiāng	急救药箱
first-aid station	jíjiù zhàn	急救站
first class (seat)	tóuděng cāng	头等舱
first run	shǒu bān chē,	首班车,头班车
(bus or train)	tóu bān chē	
fish	yú	鱼
fisherfolk	yúmín	渔民
fishing	diàoyú	钓鱼
fishing village	yúcūn	渔村
five	wǔ	五
five-grain liquor	wǔliángyè	五粮液
fix (repair)	xiūlǐ	修理
flag (n)	qí	旗
flash (camera)	shǎnguāng dēng	闪光灯
flashlight	shǒudiàntǒng	手电筒
flask	hú	壶
flight (airline)	hángbān	航班
flight schedule	hángbān shíkèbiǎo	航班时刻表
floor (of a room)	dìbǎn	地板
floor (story)	céng, lóu	层,楼
flour	miànfěn	面粉
flower	huā	花
flu	liúgǎn	流感
fluent	liúlì	流利
flute, bamboo	dízi	笛子
fly (insect)	cāngying	苍蝇
fly (v)	fēi	飞
Flying Pigeon (bike)	fēigē	飞鸽
fog	wù	雾
folder	jiāzi	夹子
folk dance	mínjiān wǔdǎo	民间舞蹈
folk music	mínjiān yīnyuè	民间音乐
folk tale	mínjiān gùshì	民间故事
folklore	mínjiān chuánshuō	民间传说
follow	gēn	跟
food	shípǐn, shíwù	食品,食物
food poisoning	shíwù zhòng dú	食物中毒
foot (12 inches)	yīngchǐ	英尺
foot (body)	jiǎo, zú	脚,足
football (American)	gǎnlǎnqiú	橄榄球

DICTIONARY

footlight	*jiǎodēng*	脚灯
footpath	*rénxíngdào*	人行道
for example	*bǐrú, bǐfang shuō*	比如,比方说
Forbidden City (Palace Museum)	*gùgōng*	故宫
foreign	*wàiguó*	外国
foreign affairs office	*wàishì bàngōngshì*	外事办公室
foreign exchange	*wàihuì*	外汇
foreign expert	*wàiguó zhuānjiā*	外国专家
foreign guest	*wàibīn*	外宾
foreign policy	*wàijiāo zhèngcè*	外交政策
foreign student	*liúxuéshēng*	留学生
foreigner	*wàiguórén*	外国人
forest	*sēnlín*	森林
Forever (bike)	*yǒngjiǔ*	永久
forget	*wàngjì*	忘记
forgive	*yuánliàng*	原谅
fork	*chāzi*	叉子
fork (road)	*chà lùkǒu*	叉路口
form (printed sheet)	*biǎogé*	表格
forty	*sìshí*	四十
forward (sports)	*qiánfēng*	前锋
four	*sì*	四
fox	*húlí*	狐狸
fracture	*gǔzhé*	骨折
fragile	*yìsuì*	易碎
fragrant	*xiāng*	香
franc	*fǎláng*	法郎
France	*fǎguó*	法国
free (no charge)	*miǎnfèi*	免费
free market	*zìyóu shìchǎng*	自由市场
freedom	*zìyóu*	自由
freelancer	*zìyóu zhíyè zhě*	自由职业者
freeze	*dòng*	冻
freezing	*bīngdòng*	冰冻
fresh	*xīnxian*	新鲜
Friday	*xīngqī wǔ*	星期五
fried, deep	*zhá*	炸
fried, lightly	*jiān*	煎
fried crisp chicken	*xiāngsū jī*	香酥鸡
fried cruller	*yóutiáo*	油条
fried dumplings (pot-stickers)	*guōtiē*	锅贴

fried egg	jiān jīdàn	煎鸡蛋
fried noodles	chǎomiàn	炒面
fried rice	chǎofàn	炒饭
fried dough twists	máhuā	麻花
friend	péngyǒu	朋友
friendship	yǒuì	友谊
Friendship Store	yǒuyì shāngdiàn	友谊商店
fries, potato	zhá shǔtiáo	炸薯条
frog	qīngwā	青蛙
front	qián	前
front door	qiánmén	前门
front section (seating)	qiánpái	前排
front yard	qiányuàn	前院
fruit	shuǐguǒ	水果
fuel	ránliào	燃料
Fuji	fùshì	富士
full	mǎn	满
full (after meal)	bǎo le	饱了
fun	yǒuqù, hǎowán	有趣, 好玩
funny (amusing)	kěxiào, dòu	可笑, 逗
fur	qiúpí, pímáo	裘皮, 皮毛
furnace	gāolú, lúzi	高炉, 炉子
furniture	jiājù	家具
fuse (n)	bǎoxiǎnsī	保险丝
gallon	jiālún	加仑
game	yóuxì	游戏
game room	yóuyì shì	游艺室
garbage can	lājī xiāng	垃圾箱
garden	huāyuán	花园
garlic	suàn	蒜
gas (coal)	méiqì	煤气
gas (vapor)	qì, qìtǐ	气, 气体
gas station	jiāyóu zhàn	加油站
gas stove	méiqìlú	煤气炉
gas tank	yóuxiāng	油箱
gasoline	qìyóu	汽油
gastric	wèi	胃
gastric perforation	wèi chuānkǒng	胃穿孔
gastritis	wèiyán	胃炎
gate	mén	门
gear (driving)	dǎng	档

DICTIONARY

gear (part)	*chǐlún*	齿轮
general anesthesia	*quánshēn mázuì*	全身麻醉
Geneva	*rìnèiwǎ*	日内瓦
geranium	*xiùqiú*	绣球花
Germany	*déguó*	德国
gesture	*dòngzuò*	动作
get (obtain)	*dé*	得
get off (a vehicle)	*xiàchē*	下车
get off work	*xiàbān*	下班
get on (a vehicle)	*shàng chē*	上车
giant panda	*dàxióngmāo*	大熊猫
gift	*lǐwù*	礼物
gin (liquor)	*dùsōngzǐ jiǔ*	杜松子酒
ginger	*shēngjiāng*	生姜
ginkgo	*yínxìng, báiguǒ*	银杏,白果
ginkgo tree	*báiguǒ shù*	白果树
ginseng	*rénshēn*	人参
girl	*nǚhái*	女孩
girlfriend	*nǚ péngyǒu*	女朋友
give	*gěi*	给
give away	*sòngdiào*	送掉
give up hope	*xièqì*	泄气
glass (cup)	*bōli bēi*	玻璃杯
glasses (optical)	*yǎnjìng*	眼镜
glassware	*bōli zhìpǐn*	玻璃制品
glaucoma	*qīngguāng yǎn*	青光眼
gloves	*shǒutào*	手套
glucose	*pútáo táng*	葡萄糖
glue (mucilage)	*jiāoshuǐ*	胶水
glue (paste)	*jiànghu*	浆糊
glutinous rice cake	*niángāo*	年糕
go (board game)	*wéiqí*	围棋
go (v)	*qù*	去
Go! (sports)	*jiā yóu*	加油!
go around (an obstacle)	*ràokāi*	绕开
go away	*zǒukāi*	走开
goalie (sports)	*shǒuményuán*	守门员
goat	*shānyáng*	山羊
gold	*jīn*	金
golden-haired monkey	*jīsīhóu*	金丝猴
goldfish	*jīnyú*	金鱼
golf	*gāoěrfū*	高尔夫

gong	*luó*	锣
good	*hǎo*	好
good luck	*hǎo yùnqi*	好运气
good morning	*zǎoshànghǎo*	早上好
good-bye	*zàijiàn*	再见
good-looking	*hǎokàn*	好看
goods (stock)	*huò*	货
goose	*é*	鹅
gorge	*xiá*	峡
government	*zhèngfǔ*	政府
grade school	*xiǎoxué*	小学
graduate (v)	*bìyè*	毕业
grain (crop)	*liángshi*	粮食
gram	*kè*	克
grammar	*yǔfǎ*	语法
Grand Canal	*dàyùnhé*	大运河
granddaughter	*sūnnǚ, wài sūnnǚ*	孙女,外孙女
grandfather (maternal)	*lǎoye, wàigōng*	姥爷,外公
grandfather (paternal)	*yéye*	爷爷
grandmother (maternal)	*lǎolao, wàipó*	姥姥,外婆
grandmother (paternal)	*nǎinai*	奶奶
grandson	*sūnzi, wàisūn*	孙子,外孙
grape	*pútáo*	葡萄
grasp (v)	*zhuā*	抓
grassland	*cǎoyuán*	草原
gray	*huīsè*	灰色
Great!	*zhēn bàng*	真棒!
Great Hall of the People	*rénmín dàhuìtáng*	人民大会堂
Great Wall	*chángchéng*	长城
Greece	*xīlà*	希腊
green	*lǜ*	绿
green onion	*dàcōng*	大葱
green tea	*lǜchá*	绿茶
greeting card	*hèkǎ*	贺卡
grilled	*kǎo*	烤
groceries	*shípǐn*	食品
grocery store	*shípìn diàn*	食品店
grotto	*shíkū*	石窟
ground (n)	*dì*	地
ground meat	*ròumò*	肉末
group (people)	*tuántǐ, qún*	团体,群
group visa	*jítǐ qiānzhèng*	集体签证

DICTIONARY

grow (plant)	zhòng	种
guarantee	bǎozhèng	保证
guard (sports)	hòuwèi	后卫
guesthouse	bīnguǎn, zhāodàisuǒ	宾馆，招待所
guide (person)	dǎoyóu	导游
guidebook	dǎoyóu shū	导游书
guitar	jíta	吉他
guitar, 3-string	sānxián qín	三弦琴
gun	qiāng	枪
gymnasium	tǐyùguǎn	体育馆
gymnastics	tǐcāo	体操
gynecologist	fùkē yīshēng	妇科医生
gynecology department	fùkē	妇科
Haagen-Dazs	hāgēndásī	哈根达斯
habit (custom)	xíguàn	习惯
hair	tóufa	头发
hair oil	fàyóu	发油
hairbrush	tóushuā	头刷
haircut	lǐfà	理发
hairspray	dìngxíng yè	定型液
half	yíbàn, bànge	一半，半个
half a day	bàntiān	半天
half-price	bànjià	半价
halt	zhànzhù	站住
ham	huǒtuǐ	火腿
hammer	chuízi	锤子
hand (n)	shǒu	手
hand carry-on	suíshēn xíngli	随身行李
hand towel	shǒujīn	手巾
hand wash	shǒu xǐ	手洗
handball	shǒuqiú	手球
handicraft	shǒugōngyì pǐn	手工艺品
handkerchief	shǒujuàn	手绢
handlebar (bike)	chēbǎ	车把
handmade	shǒugōng zhìzuò	手工制作
happen	fāshēng	发生
happiness	xìngfú	幸福
happiness (symbol)	xǐ	喜
harbor	gǎng	港
hard-seat	yìngzuò	硬座

hard-sleeper	yìngwò	硬卧
harvest (n)	shōuhuò	收获
hat	màozi	帽子
hate	hèn	恨
have	yǒu	有
haw	shānzhā	山楂
Hawaii	xiàwēiyí	夏威夷
hay fever	huāfěn rè	花粉热
he	tā	他
head	tóu	头
headache	tóuténg	头疼
headlight	qiándēng	前灯
health	jiànkāng	健康
health care	bǎojiàn	保健
health club	jiànshēn fáng	健身房
health declaration	jiànkāng biǎo	健康表
heart	xīnzhàng, xīn	心脏,心
heart attack	xīnzàngbìng fāzuò	心脏病发作
heat (energy)	rèliàng, rè	热量,热
heat (radiator)	nuǎnqì	暖气
heat (v)	jiārè	加热
heavy	chén, zhòng	沉, 重
heavy (taste)	nóng	浓
hectare	gōngqǐng	公顷
hedge rose	qiángwēi	蔷薇
height	gāo dù	高度
hello	nǐhǎo	你好
help (n)	bāngzhù	帮助
help (v)	bāng	帮
Helsinki	hèěrxīnjī	赫尔辛基
hemorrhage	chūxuè	出血
Henan Opera	yùjù	豫剧
hepatitis	gānyán	肝炎
her	tāde	她的
herbal medicine	cǎoyào	草药
here	zhèli, zhèr	这里, 这儿
hero	yīngxióng	英雄
heroin	hǎiluòyīn	海洛因
heroine	nǚ yīngxióng	女英雄
hesitation	yóuyù	犹豫
hey	wèi	喂
high	gāo	高

DICTIONARY

high school	zhōngxué	中学
highest	zuì gāo	最高
highland	gāoyuán	高原
highway	gōnglù	公路
hiking	túbùlǚxíng	徒步旅行
hiking boot	yuǎnzúxié	远足鞋
hill	shān	山
Hilton	xīěrdùn	希尔顿
Himalayas	xǐmǎlāyǎ shān	喜玛拉雅山
hip	kuà	胯
hire (a person)	gù	雇
hire (charter)	bāo	包
hired car	bāochē	包车
his	tāde	他的
history	lìshǐ	历史
history museum	lìshǐ bówùguǎn	历史博物馆
HIV	àizībìngbìngdú	艾滋病病毒
hold (embrace)	bào	抱
hold (take)	názhe	拿着
holder	jiàzi	架子
holiday	jiérì	节日
Hollywood	hǎoláiwū	好莱坞
home	jiā	家
home-style	jiācháng	家常
homemaker	zhǔfù	主妇
Honda	běntián	本田
honey crystallized apples	básī píngguǒ	拔丝苹果
Hong Kong	xiānggǎng	香港
Hong Kong dollar	gǎngbì	港币
honor	róngxìng	荣幸
hook (n)	gōuzi	钩子
hope	xīwàng	希望
horrible	kěpà	可怕
hors d'oeuvre	lěngpán	冷盘
horse	mǎ	马
hospital	yīyuàn	医院
hospitality	hàokè, kuǎndài	好客，款待
host (person)	zhǔrén	主人
host organization	jiēdài dānwèi	接待单位
hostel	lǚshè	旅社
hot	rè	热

hot (spicy)	là	辣
hot-and-sour soup	suānlà tāng	酸辣汤
hot pot	huǒguō	火锅
hot sauce	làjiàng	辣酱
hot spring	wēnquán	温泉
hot water (from tap)	rèshuǐ	热水
hotel	lǚguǎn, fàndiàn	旅馆，饭店
hour	xiǎoshí	小时
house	fángzi	房子
housekeeping department	kèfáng bù	客房部
how	zěnme	怎么
how far	duōyuǎn	多远
how long (length)	duōcháng	多长
how long (time)	duōjiǔ	多久
how many	jǐgè, duōshao	几个，多少
how much	duōshao	多少
how old (person)	duōdà	多大
humid	cháoshī	潮湿
humor	yōumò	幽默
humor, sense of	yōumò gǎn	幽默感
hundred	bǎi	百
hundred million	yì	亿
hunting	dǎliè	打猎
hurry up	gǎnkuài	赶快
hurt	téng	疼
husband	zhàngfu, àirén	丈夫，爱人
Hyatt	kǎiyuè	凯乐
hypertension	gāo xuèyā	高血压
hypodermic	píxià	皮下
hypotension	dī xuèyā	低血压
I	wǒ	我
ice	bīng	冰
ice cream	bīngqílín	冰淇淋
ice hockey	bīngqiú	冰球
ice water	bīngshuǐ	冰水
idea	zhúyì, xiǎngfǎ	主意，想法
idiom	chéngyǔ	成语
if	rúguǒ	如果
illness	bìng	病
image	xíngxiàng	形象

DICTIONARY

imitate	*mófǎng*	模仿
immediately	*mǎshàng*	马上
immigrant	*yímín*	移民
immigration checkpoint	*yímín jiǎnchá zhàn*	移民检查站
implement (a policy)	*zhíxíng*	执行
import	*jìnkǒu*	进口
import goods	*jìnkǒu huò*	进口货
import license	*jìnkǒu xǔkězhèng*	进口许可证
important	*zhòngyào*	重要
impression (thought)	*yìnxiàng*	印象
inch (n)	*yīngcùn*	英寸
increase	*zēngjiā*	增加
India	*yìndù*	印度
indigestion	*xiāohuà bù liáng*	消化不良
individual	*gèrén, gètǐ*	个人，个体
industry	*gōngyè, chǎnyè*	工业，产业
inexpensive	*búguì*	不贵
infection	*fāyán*	发炎
infectious	*chuánrǎn*	传染
inflammation	*fāyán*	发炎
information (knowledge)	*zhīshi*	知识
information (news)	*xiāoxi*	消息
information desk	*wènxùn chù*	问讯处
injection	*zhùshè, dǎzhēn*	注射，打针
ink (for calligraphy)	*mòzhī*	墨汁
ink (for fountain pen)	*mòshuǐ*	墨水
ink painting, Chinese	*shuǐmò huà*	水墨画
ink slab	*yàntai*	砚台
ink stick	*mò*	墨
Inner Mongolia	*nèiměnggǔ*	内蒙古
inner tube (wheel)	*nèitāi*	内胎
inpatient department	*zhùyuàn chù*	住院处
inquire	*xúnwèn*	询问
insect	*kūnchóng*	昆虫
inside	*lǐmiàn*	里面
insignia (badge)	*huīzhāng*	徽章
insomnia	*shīmián*	失眠
instrumental music	*qìyuè*	器乐
insure	*bǎoxiǎn*	保险
intellectual	*zhīshi fènzǐ*	知识分子
intelligent	*cōngmíng*	聪明

interesting	yǒu yìsi	有意思
intermission	mùjiān xiūxi	幕间休息
intern	shíxí shēng	实习生
internal	nèi	内
international	guójì	国际
Internet	hùliánwǎng, yīntèwǎng	互联网，因特网
Internet cafe	wǎngbā	网吧
interpreter	fānyì	翻译
intersection (crossroad)	shízì lùkǒu	十字路口
intravenous injection	jìngmài zhùshè	静脉注射
introduction	jièshào	介绍
inventor	fāmíngzhě	发明者
investigate	diàochá	调查
invitation card	qǐngtiě	请贴
iron (for clothing)	yùndǒu	熨斗
iron (metal)	tiě	铁
iron (v)	yùn, tàng	熨，烫
Iron Goddess of Mercy tea	tiěguānyīn chá	铁观音茶
iron openwork	tiěhuā	铁花
is	shì	是
island	dǎo	岛
isolation ward	gélí bìngfáng	隔离病房
it	tā	它
It's a pity.	hěn yíhàn	很遗憾。
It's nothing.	méi guānxi	没关系。
Italian opera	yìdàlì gējù	意大利歌剧
Italy	yìdàlì	意大利
itch	yǎng	痒
itinerary	rìchéng	日程
IUD	gōng nèi bìyùnqì	宫内避孕器
ivory	xiàngyá	象牙
ivory carving	yádiāo	牙雕
jacket	jiākè	夹克
jade	yù	玉
jade carving	yùdiāo	玉雕
jade carving factory	yùdiāo chǎng	玉雕厂
jadeite	fěicuì	翡翠
jail	jiānyù	监狱
jam (jelly)	guǒjiàng	果酱
January	yīyuè	一月

DICTIONARY

Japan	rìběn	日本
Japanese yen	rìyuán	日元
jar	píng, guàn	瓶，罐
jasmine tea	mòlì huāchá	茉莉花茶
jaw	xiàba	下巴
jaywalking	luàn chuān mǎlù	乱穿马路
jazz music	juéshìyuè	爵士乐
jeep	jípǔchē	吉普车
jellyfish	hǎizhé	海蜇
jet lag	shíchā fǎnyìng	时差反应
jewel (precious)	zhūbǎo	珠宝
jewelry (ornamental)	shǒushì	首饰
job	gōngzuò	工作
join	cānjiā	参加
joints (body)	guānjié	关节
joke (v)	kāi wánxiào	开玩笑
journal (diary)	rìjì	日记
journal (periodical)	qīkān, kānwù	期刊，刊物
journalism	xīnwén gōngzuò	新闻工作
journalist (reporter)	jìzhě	记者
judge (n)	fáguān	法官
judge (v)	pànduàn	判断
judo	róudào	柔道
juice (fruit)	guǒzhī	果汁
July	qīyuè	七月
jump	tiào, bèng	跳，蹦
jump rope (n)	tiàoshéng	跳绳
June	liùyuè	六月
jungle	cónglín	丛林
just	jiù	就
just now	cái, gāngcái	才，刚才
karst	yánróng	岩溶
Keemun tea	qímén hóngchá	祁门红茶
keep	bǎoliú	保留
ketchup (catsup)	fānqié jiàng	蕃茄酱
key (n)	yàoshi	钥匙
keyboard instrument	jiànpán yuèqì	健盘乐器
kick (v)	tī	踢
kidney	shèn	肾
kidney bean	yúndòu	云豆
kidskin	xiǎoshānyáng pí	小山羊皮

Kiev	*jīfǔ*	基辅
kill (v)	*shā*	杀
kilogram	*gōngjīn*	公斤
kilometer	*gōnglǐ*	公里
kind (personality)	*shànliáng*	善良
kindergarten	*yòuéryuán*	幼儿园
kiss (n)	*qīn, wěn*	亲，吻
kitchen	*chúfáng*	厨房
kite	*fēngzheng*	风筝
knee	*xīgài*	膝盖
knife	*dāozi*	刀子
knit	*zhī*	织
know (a fact)	*zhīdao*	知道
know (a person)	*rènshì*	认识
know how to	*huì*	会
knowledge	*zhīshi*	知识
Kodak	*kēdá*	柯达
Korea	*cháoxiǎn*	朝鲜
Kowloon	*jiǔlóng*	九龙
Kublai Khan	*hūbìliè*	忽必烈
kumquat	*jīnjú*	金桔
Kunshan Opera	*kūnqǔ*	昆曲
Kyoto	*jīngdū*	京都
label (n)	*biāoqiān*	标签
labor union	*gōnghuì*	工会
laboratory	*huàyàn shì*	化验室
lacquer, carved	*diāoqī*	雕漆
lacquerware	*qīqì*	漆器
lake	*hú*	湖
lamasery	*lǎmasì*	喇嘛寺
lamb (mutton)	*yángròu*	羊肉
lambskin	*xiǎoyáng pí*	小羊皮
lamp	*dēng*	灯
land (earth)	*tǔdì*	土地
landscape	*fēngjǐng*	风景
landslide	*shānbēng*	山崩
lane	*hútong, xiàng*	胡同，巷
language	*yǔyán*	语言
large	*dà*	大
largest	*zuìdà*	最大
last (final)	*zuìhòu*	最后

DICTIONARY

last month	shàng ge yuè	上个月
last one	zuìhòu yígè	最后一个
last run (bus or train)	mòbān chē	末班车
last week	shàng ge xīngqī	上个星期
last year	qùnián	去年
later (afterwards)	hòulái	后来
later (in a while)	yíhuìr	一会儿
laundry (clean)	xǐ wán de yīfu	洗完的衣服
laundry (dirty)	yào xǐ de yīfu	要洗的衣服
laundry bag	xǐyīdài	洗衣袋
laundry detergent	xǐyīfěn	洗衣粉
law	fǎlù	法律
lawyer	lùshī	律师
layered	duōcéng	多层
lazy	lǎn	懒
lead (v)	dài, lǐng	带，领
lead actor (or actress)	zhǔyǎn	主演
leader	lǐngdǎo	领导
leads to (street)	tōngxiàng	通向
leaf	shùyè	树叶
leak (v)	lòu	漏
lean (thin)	shòu	瘦
leopard	bào	豹
learn	xué	学
leather	pígé	皮革
leather shoes	píxié	皮鞋
leave (behind)	liú	留
leave (depart)	líkāi	离开
leave (set out)	chūfā	出发
leave a message (spoken)	liú huà	留话
leave a note	liú tiáo	留条
lecture (n)	jiǎngzuò	讲座
left (direction)	zuǒ	左
left luggage office	xíngli jìcúnchù	行李寄存处
leg	tuǐ	腿
lemon	níngméng	柠檬
lemonade	níngméng shuǐ	柠檬水
length	chángdù	长度
Leningrad	shèngbǐdébǎo	圣彼德堡
lens (camera)	jìngtóu	镜头
less	shǎo	少

lesser panda	*xiǎoxióngmāo*	小熊猫
lesson (class)	*kè*	课
lesson (moral)	*jiàoxùn*	教训
let	*ràng*	让
letter (mail)	*xìn*	信
lettuce	*wōjù*	莴苣
level (degree)	*shuǐpíng*	水平
Lijiang River	*líjiāng*	漓江
liberalism	*zìyóuhuà*	自由化
library	*túshūguǎn*	图书馆
lice	*shīzi*	虱子
license plate	*chēpái*	车牌
lie down	*tǎng xià*	躺下
life	*shēnghuó*	生活
light (in color, density)	*qiǎn, dàn*	浅，淡
light (lamp)	*dēng*	灯
light (to kindle)	*diǎn*	点
light (weight)	*qīng*	轻
light bulb	*dēngpào*	灯泡
light meter	*cèguāng biǎo*	测光表
lighting	*zhàomíng*	照明
lighting design	*dēngguāng shèjì*	灯光设计
like (v)	*xǐhuān*	喜欢
like this (this way)	*zhèyàng*	这样
lilac	*dīngxiāng*	丁香
line (n)	*xiàn*	线
linen	*yàmá bù*	亚麻布
linguistics	*yǔyánxué*	语言学
lion	*shīzi*	狮子
lion dance	*shīzi wǔ*	狮子舞
liquor	*jiǔ*	酒
lira	*lǐlā*	里拉
listen to	*tīng*	听
listen to music	*tīng yīnyuè*	听音乐
liter	*shēng*	升
literature	*wénxué*	文学
lithograph	*shíbǎnhuà*	石板画
little (small)	*xiǎo*	小
live (reside)	*zhù*	住
live telecast	*xiànchǎng zhíbō*	现场直播
liver	*gān*	肝
living	*huózhe*	活着

DICTIONARY

living room	*kètīng*	客厅
lobby (n)	*xiūxishì*	休息室
lobster	*lóngxiā*	龙虾
local (place)	*dìfāng*	地方
local (slow bus or train)	*mànchē*	慢车
local (within a city)	*běndì, dāngdì*	本地，当地
local anesthesia	*júbù mázuì*	局部麻醉
local guide	*dìpéi*	地陪
local money, Chinese	*rénmínbì*	人民币
local opera	*dìfāng xì*	地方戏
located at	*zài*	在
location	*dìdiǎn*	地点
lock	*suǒ*	锁
lock (ship)	*chuánzhá*	船闸
locust tree	*huáishù*	槐树
London	*lúndūn*	伦敦
lonely	*jìmò*	寂寞
long (adj)	*cháng*	长
long-distance	*chángtú*	长途
long-distance bus	*chángtú qìchē*	长途汽车
long live...	*...wànsuì*	……万岁
longan fruit	*lóngyǎn*	龙眼
longevity	*chángshòu*	长寿
longevity (symbol)	*shòu*	寿
look	*kàn*	看
loose	*sōngsǎn*	松散
loquat	*pípá*	枇杷
Los Angeles	*luòshānjī*	洛杉矶
lose	*diūshī*	丢失
lost (an object)	*diū le*	丢了
lost (the way)	*mílù*	迷路
lost-and-found office	*shīwù zhāolǐng chù*	失物招领处
lotus flower	*liánhuā, héhuā*	莲花，荷花
lotus root	*ǒu*	藕
lotus seed	*liánzǐ*	莲子
loud	*dàshēng*	大声
love (n)	*àiqíng*	爱情
love (v)	*ài*	爱
low	*dī*	低
low/high blood pressure	*xuěyā guòdī / guògāo*	血压过低 / 过高
lowest	*zuìdī*	最低
luck	*yùnqi*	运气

luck (symbol)	fú	福
luggage (see baggage)	xíngli	行李
luggage rack	xíngli jià	行李架
lumbago	yāoténg	腰疼
lunch (n)	wǔfàn	午饭
lung	fèi	肺
lute, 4-string	pípá	琵琶
lychee (litchi)	lìzhī	荔枝
lynx	shěli	猞猁
lyric (song)	gēcí	歌词
Macao	àomén	澳门
machine	jīqì	机器
Madrid	mǎdélǐ	马德里
magazine (reading)	zázhì	杂志
magic	móshù	魔术
magician	móshùshī	魔术师
mah-jong	májiàng	麻将
mail (letters)	xìn	信
mail (v)	jì	寄
mailbox	yóutǒng	邮筒
main	zhǔyào	主要
main character	zhǔjié	主角
main desk	zǒngtái	总台
maître d'	zǒngguǎn	总管
make	zuò	做
make progress	yǒu jìnzhǎn	有进展
make-up (cosmetics)	huàzhuāng	化妆
malaria	nüèji	疟疾
male (animals)	gōng, xióng	公，雄
male (people)	nán	男
man	nánrén	男人
management	guǎnlǐ	管理
manager	jīnglǐ	经理
Manchurian jasper	xiùyù	岫玉
mandarin ducks	yuānyang	鸳鸯
mandarin orange	gānzi	柑子
mandolin, 4-string	yuèqín	月琴
mango	mángguǒ	芒果
manicure	xiū zhǐjia	修指甲
manual transmission (car)	shǒudòng huàndǎng	手动换档
manual worker	gōngrén	工人

DICTIONARY

manufacture (produce)	shēngchǎn	生产
many	hǎo duō	好多
Mao cap	jūnmào	军帽
Mao jacket	jūnbiànfú	军便服
Maotai liquor	máotái	茅台
map (n)	dìtú	地图
marble	dàlǐshí	大理石
March	sānyuè	三月
Marco Polo	mǎkě bōluó	马可·波罗
marijuana	dàmá	大麻
marine (military)	hǎijūn lùzhànduì	海军陆战队
marionette	tíxiàn mùǒu	提线木偶
mark (currency)	mǎkè	马克
marriage	hūnyīn	婚姻
marry	jiéhūn	结婚
marten	diāo	貂
martial arts	wǔshù	武术
martial arts performer	wǔshù biǎoyǎnzhě	武术表演者
martyr	lièshì	烈士
mashed potatoes	tǔdòu ní	土豆泥
mask	miànjù	面具
massage	ànmó, tuīná	按摩，推拿
masses (people)	qúnzhòng	群众
master worker	shīfu	师傅
matches	huǒchái	火柴
maternity ward	chǎnkē bìngfáng	产科病房
mathematics	shùxué	数学
matter (affair)	shìqing	事情
mattress	chuángdiàn	床垫
mausoleum	líng	陵
Maxwell House	màishì	麦氏
May	wǔyuè	五月
maybe	yěxǔ	也许
me	wǒ	我
meaning	yìsi	意思
measles	mázhěn	麻疹
measure (v)	cèliáng	测量
meatball	ròu wánzi	肉丸子
mechanic	jìgōng	技工
medical science	yīxué	医学
medicine	yīyào	医药
medicine, traditional Chinese, TCM	zhōngyī	中医

medium (size)	*zhōng hào*	中号
meet (a person)	*jiàn*	见
meeting (n)	*huì*	会
Melbourne	*Mò ěrběn*	墨尔本
melon, Hami	*hāmìguā*	哈密瓜
member (of a group)	*chénguán*	成员
memorial arch	*páilou*	牌楼
memorial hall	*jìniàntáng*	纪念堂
memory	*jìyì*	记忆
men's bike	*nánchē*	男车
mend	*bǔ*	补
meningitis	*nǎomó yán*	脑膜炎
menstruation	*yuèjīng*	月经
mental	*jīngshén*	精神
menu	*càidān*	菜单
Mercedes Benz	*bēnchí*	奔驰
merchandise	*shāngpǐn*	商品
metal	*jīnshǔ*	金属
meter (metric)	*mǐ*	米
meter (taxi)	*jìjiàqì*	计价器
method	*fāngfǎ*	方法
metric ton	*gōngdūn*	公吨
Mickey Mouse	*mǐlǎoshǔ*	米老鼠
microphone	*huàtǒng*	话筒
midnight	*bànyè*	半夜
migraine	*piān tóuténg*	偏头疼
mile	*yīnglǐ*	英里
military	*jūnshì*	军事
military band	*jūnyuèduì*	军乐队
milk	*niúnǎi*	牛奶
Milky Way	*yínhé*	银河
milliliter	*háoshēng*	毫升
millimeter	*háomǐ*	毫米
million	*bǎiwàn*	百万
mind (brain)	*tóunǎo*	头脑
mine (my)	*wǒde*	我的
mineral water	*kuàngquán shuǐ*	矿泉水
Ming Tombs	*shísānlíng*	十三陵
mini-bus	*miànbāochē*	面包车
miniature bottle painting	*bíyānhú*	鼻烟壶
miniature carving	*wēidiāo*	微雕
mink	*shuǐdiāo*	水貂

DICTIONARY

Minolta	*měinéngdá*	美能达
minorities' dance	*mínzú wǔdǎo*	民族舞蹈
minute (n)	*fēnzhōng*	分钟
mirror (n)	*jìngzi*	镜子
miscarriage	*liúchǎn*	流产
miscellaneous	*záwù, záshì*	杂务，杂事
mischievous	*táoqì*	淘气
Miss	*xiǎojiě*	小姐
mistake (n)	*cuòwù*	错误
mistake (v)	*nòngcuò, gǎocuò*	弄错，搞错
Mitsubishi	*sānlíng*	三菱
Mobile phone	*shǒujī*	手机
Mocha	*mókǎ*	摩卡
model (of an object)	*móxíng*	模型
model (person)	*mótèr*	模特儿
modern (advanced)	*xiàndài*	现代
modern (style)	*xiàndàipài*	现代派
modernization	*xiàndàihuà*	现代化
monastery	*sì, sìyuàn*	寺，寺院
Monday	*xīngqī yī*	星期一
money	*qián*	钱
money order	*huìpiào*	汇票
Mongolian hot pot	*shuànyángròu*	涮羊肉
monk	*héshàng*	和尚
monkey	*hóuzi*	猴子
monster	*móguǐ, guàiwù*	魔鬼，怪物
month	*yuè*	月
monthly ticket (bus, subway)	*yuèpiào*	月票
monument	*jìniànbēi*	纪念碑
moon	*yuèliang, yuè*	月亮，月
mop (n)	*tuōbǎ*	拖把
mop (v)	*tuōdì*	拖地
more	*duō*	多
morning	*zǎochén, shàngwǔ*	早晨，上午
morphine	*mǎfēi*	吗啡
Moscow	*mòsīkē*	莫斯科
Moslem	*mùsilín*	穆斯林
mosque	*qīngzhēn sì*	清真寺
mosquito	*wénzi*	蚊子
mosquito coil	*wén xiāng*	蚊香
most (comparative)	*zuì*	最

most (majority of)	dà duōshù	大多数
mother	mǔqīn	母亲
motor	mǎdá	马达
Mount Qomolangma	zhūmùlángmǎ fēng	珠穆朗玛峰
mountain	shān	山
mountain bike	shāndìchē	山地车
mountaineering	dēngshān	登山
mountain range	shānmài	山脉
mounting	zhuāngbiǎo	装裱
mouth	zuǐ	嘴
mouth organ, Chinese	shēng	笙
mouthwash	shùkǒu jì	漱口剂
move aside (objects)	bānkāi	搬开
move aside (people)	ràngkāi	让开
movement (music)	yuèzhāng	乐章
movie	diànyǐng	电影
movie camera	diànyǐng shèxiàngjī	电影摄像机
movie star	yǐngxīng	影星
Mr.	xiānsheng	先生
Mrs.	tàitai, fūrén	太太，夫人
Ms.	nǚshì	女士
MSG	wèijīng	味精
much	duō	多
mug	bēizi	杯子
mulberry tree	sāngshù	桑树
multiply	chéng	乘
mung bean	lùdòu	绿豆
mural	bìhuà	壁画
muscle	jīròu	肌肉
museum	bówùguǎn	博物馆
mushroom	mógu	蘑菇
music	yīnyuè	音乐
musical (show)	gēwǔjù	歌舞剧
musical instrument	yuèqì	乐器
musical staff, 5-line	wǔxiànpǔ	五线谱
Muslim food	qīngzhēncài	清真菜
must	bìxū	必须
mustard (condiment)	jièmo	芥末
mustard, leaf	gàicài	芥菜
musty	fāméi	发霉
mutton	yángròu	羊肉
my	wǒde	我的

DICTIONARY

Myanmar	*miǎndiàn*	缅甸
My God!	*wǒde tiān*	我的天!
nail (hardware)	*dīngzi*	钉子
name (n)	*míngzi*	名字
napkin, paper	*cānjīnzhǐ*	餐巾纸
narcissus	*shuǐxiān*	水仙
narrow	*xiázhǎi*	狭窄
nasal congestion	*bízi bù tōng*	鼻子不通
national (adj)	*guójiā*	国家
national anthem	*guógē*	国歌
national defense	*guófáng*	国防
national emblem	*guóhuī*	国徽
national flag	*guóqí*	国旗
national guide	*quánpéi*	全陪
nationality (ethnic)	*mínzú*	民族
national park	*guójiā gōngyuán*	国家公园
native place (ancestral)	*lǎojiā*	老家
natural	*zìrán*	自然
natural reserve	*zìrán bǎohù qū*	自然保护区
nature (character)	*xìnggé*	性格
nature (outdoors)	*dà zìrán*	大自然
nauseous	*ěxīn*	恶心
navy	*hǎijūn*	海军
near	*jìn*	近
nearest	*zuìjìn*	最近
neck	*bózi*	脖子
necklace	*xiàngliàn*	项链
need	*xūyào, yào*	需要，要
needle	*zhēn*	针
needle and thread	*zhēnxiàn*	针线
needlework	*zhēnxiàn huó*	针线活
negative (film)	*dǐpiàn*	底片
neighbor	*línjū*	邻居
Neolithic era	*xīn shíqì shídài*	新石器时代
Nepal	*níbóěr*	尼泊尔
nerve	*shénjīng*	神经
nervous (mood)	*jǐnzhāng*	紧张
Nescafe	*quècáo*	雀巢
Netherlands	*hélán*	荷兰
neurology	*shénjīngbìngxué*	神经病学
neurosis	*shénjíngzhèng*	神经症

never	*yǒngbù*	永不
never again	*zài yě bù*	再也不
never have	*cóng méi*	从没
new	*xīn*	新
New Wave	*xīncháo*	新潮
New Year	*xīnnián, yuándàn*	新年，元旦
New Year painting	*niánhuà*	年画
New York	*niǔyuē*	纽约
New Zealand	*xīnxīlán*	新西兰
New Zealand dollar	*xīnxīlán yuán*	新西兰元
news	*xīnwén, xiāoxi*	新闻，消息
news program	*xīnwén jiémù*	新闻节目
newspaper	*bàozhǐ*	报纸
newsstand	*bàotíng, bàotān*	报亭，报摊
next (forthcoming)	*xiàyígè, xiàmiànde*	下一个，下面的
next stop	*xiàzhàn*	下站
next time	*xiàcì*	下次
next to (at the side of)	*zài...pángbiān*	在……旁边
next year	*míngnián*	明年
nice	*hǎo, bú cuò*	好，不错
night	*yèwǎn*	夜晚
night bus	*yèbānchē*	夜班车
night market	*yèshì*	夜市
night shift	*yèbān*	夜班
nightlife	*yèshēnghuó*	夜生活
nightstand	*chuángtóuguì*	床头柜
Nikon	*níkāng*	尼康
nine	*jiǔ*	九
ninety	*jiǔshí*	九十
Nissan	*nísāng*	尼桑
noisy	*chǎo*	吵
nomadic people	*yóumù mínzú*	游牧民族
nonsmoking	*jìnyān*	禁烟
nonstaple food	*fùshípǐn*	副食品
noodles	*miàntiáo*	面条
noon	*zhōngwǔ*	中午
north	*běi*	北
North America	*běiměizhōu*	北美洲
North Pole	*běijí*	北极
North Star	*běijí xīng*	北极星
nose	*bízi*	鼻子
not	*bù, méi*	不，没

DICTIONARY

not bad	*bú cuò*	不错
notebook	*bǐjìběn*	笔记本
novel (n)	*xiǎoshuō*	小说
November	*shíyīyuè*	十一月
now	*xiànzài*	现在
nuclear	*hé*	核
numb	*má*	麻
number (numeral)	*hàomǎ*	号码
number (quantity)	*shùzi*	数字
nurse (n)	*hùshì*	护士
nursery school	*tuōérsuǒ*	托儿所
o'clock	*diǎnzhōng*	点钟
oatmeal	*màipiàn*	麦片
object (thing)	*dōngxi*	东西
observation ward	*guānchá shì*	观察室
ocean	*hǎiyáng*	海洋
October	*shíyuè*	十月
of course	*dāngrán*	当然
office	*bàngōngshì*	办公室
office worker	*zhíyuán*	职员
often	*jīngcháng*	经常
Oh well (forget it)	*suànle*	算了
oil	*yóu*	油
oil (petroleum)	*shíyóu*	石油
oil painting	*yóuhuà*	油画
ointment	*ruǎngāo*	软膏
okay	*xíng*	行
old (aged)	*lǎo*	老
old (used)	*jiù*	旧
old age	*lǎonián*	老年
old man	*lǎo dàye*	老大爷
old town (section of a city)	*lǎochéng, jiùchéng*	老城，旧城
oleander	*jiāzhútáo*	夹竹桃
olive	*gǎnlǎn*	橄榄
Olympic Games	*àoyùnhuì*	奥运会
omelet	*dànjiǎo*	蛋饺
on holiday	*dùjià*	度假
one	*yī*	一
one-child policy	*dúshēng zǐnǚ zhèngcè*	独生子女政策
one-way street	*dānxíng xiàn*	单行线

one-way ticket	dānchéng piào	单程票
onion	cōngtóu	葱头
only	zhǐ	只
oolong tea	wūlóng chá	乌龙茶
open	kāi	开
open-dated ticket	bú dìngqī piào	不定期票
open for business	kāimén	开门
opera	gējù	歌剧
opera mask	xìjù liǎnpǔ	戏剧脸谱
opera singer (Chinese opera)	xìjù yǎnyuán	戏剧演员
opera singer	gējù yǎnyuán	歌剧演员
operation room	shǒushù shì	手术室
operator (phone)	zǒngjī	总机
ophthalmologist	yǎnkē yīshēng	眼科医生
ophthalmology department	yǎn kē	眼科
opinion	yìjiàn	意见
opium	yāpiàn	鸦片
opportunity	jīhuì	机会
or	huòzhě, háishì	或者，还是
orange (color)	júhuáng	桔黄
orange (fruit)	gānjú, chéng	柑桔，橙
orange juice	chéngzhī	橙汁
orange soda	júzi shuǐ	桔子水
orchestra	jiāoxiǎngyuè duì	交响乐队
orchestra, traditional Chinese	mínzú yuèduì	民族乐队
orchid	lánhuā	兰花
order (command)	mìnglìng	命令
order (for purchase)	dìnggòu	订购
order (sequence)	cìxù	次序
order food	diǎncài	点菜
original (n)	yuánzuò, yuánjiàn	原作，原件
ornament	zhuāngshì	装饰
other	biéde	别的
otter	shuǐtǎ	水獭
ounce	àngsī	盎司
our	wǒmende	我们的
outlet (electrical)	chāzuò	插座
outside	wàimiàn	外面
outstanding	chūsè	出色

DICTIONARY

English	Pinyin	Chinese
overcoat	dàyī	大衣
overpass	tiānqiáo	天桥
overseas Chinese	huáqiáo	华侨
overseas edition	hǎiwàibǎn	海外版
overture (music)	xùqǔ	序曲
overworked (tired)	láolèi	劳累
owe	qiàn	欠
own	yǒu	有
ox	niú	牛
oxygen	yǎngqì	氧气
oyster	háo	蚝
oyster sauce	háoyóu	蚝油
Pacific Ocean	tàipíngyáng	太平洋
pack (v)	zhuāng	装
pack suitcases	dǎ xíngli	打行李
package (n)	bāoguǒ	包裹
packaging tape	mìfēngjiāodài	密封胶带
pagoda	tǎ	塔
paid	yǐfù	已付
pain (physical)	téng	疼
pain-killer	zhǐténgyào	止疼药
paint (a picture)	huàhuà	画画
painter (artist)	huàjiā	画家
painting (art)	huìhuà	绘画
painting, traditional Chinese	guóhuà	国画
pajama	shuìyī	睡衣
palace	gōngdiàn	宫殿
palpitation	xīnjì	心悸
pancake (for Peking duck)	báobǐng	薄饼
panda	xióngmāo	熊猫
pantomime	yǎjù	哑剧
pants	kùzi	裤子
paper	zhǐ	纸
paper clip	zhǐjiā	纸夹
papercut (folk art)	jiǎnzhǐ	剪纸
parade (military)	yuèbīng	阅兵
parasol tree, Chinese	wútóngshù	梧桐树
parcel	bāoguǒ	包裹
pardon (an offense)	ráoshù	饶恕

parents	*fùmǔ*	父母
Paris	*bālí*	巴黎
park (a vehicle)	*tíng*	停
park, public	*gōngyuán*	公园
parking lot	*tíngchēchǎng*	停车场
part (not whole)	*bùfen*	部分
partner	*huǒbàn*	伙伴
party (gathering)	*jùhuì*	聚会
party (political)	*dǎng*	党
party member	*dǎngyuán*	党员
pass (go beyond)	*guò*	过
passion	*gǎnqíng*	感情
passport	*hùzhào*	护照
past, in the	*guòqù*	过去
patience	*nàixīn*	耐心
patient (sick person)	*bìngrén*	病人
pattern (decorative)	*tú àn*	图案
pattern (standard)	*guīgé*	规格
pavilion	*tíngzi*	亭子
pay (v)	*fùqián*	付钱
pea	*wāndòu*	豌豆
pea-flour cake	*wāndòuhuáng*	豌豆黄
peace	*hépíng*	和平
peach	*táozi*	桃子
peak (mountain)	*shānfēng*	山峰
peanut	*huāshēng*	花生
pear	*lí*	梨
pearl	*zhēnzhū*	珍珠
pearl cream	*zhēnzhūshuāng*	珍珠霜
Pearl River	*zhūjiāng*	珠江
peasant	*nóngmín*	农民
pedal (n)	*jiǎotàbǎn*	脚踏板
peddler	*xiǎofàn*	小贩
pedestrian	*xíngrén*	行人
pediatrician	*érkēyīshēng*	儿科医生
pediatrics department	*érkē*	儿科
peel (n)	*pí*	皮
peel (v)	*xiāopí*	削皮
Peking duck	*běijīng kǎoyā*	北京烤鸭
pen (ball-point)	*yuánzhūbǐ*	圆珠笔
pen (fountain)	*gāngbǐ*	钢笔
pencil	*qiānbǐ*	铅笔

DICTIONARY

penicillin	qīngméisù	青霉素
peony	mǔdān	牡丹
people (of a nation)	rénmín	人民
People's Daily	rénmín rìbào	人民日报
pepper (ground)	hújiāofěn	胡椒粉
pepper, green	qīngjiāo	青椒
pepper, hot	làjiāo	辣椒
percent	bǎifēnzhī…	百分之……
percussion instrument	dǎjiyuèqì	打击乐器
performer	biǎoyǎnzhě	表演者
perfume	xiāngshuǐ	香水
perhaps	yěxǔ	也许
permanent wave	tàngfà	烫发
permission	xǔkě, yǔnxǔ	许可，允许
persimmon	shìzi	柿子
person	rén	人
personal	gèrénde, sīrénde	个人的，私人的
personal effects	sīrén cáichǎn	私人财产
personality	xìnggé	性格
petroleum	shíyóu	石油
pharmacist	yàojìshī	药剂师
pharmacy	yàofáng	药房
Philadelphia	fèichéng	费城
Philippines	fēilùbīn	菲律宾
phoenix	fènghuáng	凤凰
phone (see telephone)	diànhuà	电话
photo album	yǐngjí, xiàngcè	影集，像册
photograph (n)	zhàopiàn	照片
photograph (v)	zhàoxiàng	照相
photographer	shèyǐngshī	摄影师
photography	shèyǐng	摄影
physics	wùlǐ	物理
piano	gāngqín	钢琴
pick (select)	tiāo	挑
pick up (get)	qǔ	取
pick up (meet)	jiē	接
pick up (retrieve from ground)	jiǎn	捡
pickled cabbage, hot	làbáicài	辣白菜
pickled cucumber	suānhuángguā	酸黄瓜
pickled mustard tuber, hot	zhàcài	榨菜
pickled vegetables	pàocài	泡菜

pictorial (magazine)	huàbào	画报
picture	túhuà	图画
picture book	huàcè	画册
piece (n)	kuài, jiàn, gè	块，件，个
pig	zhū	猪
pigeon	gēzi	鸽子
pill	yàowán	药丸
pillar	zhùzi	柱子
pillow	zhěntou	枕头
pillowcase	zhěntoutào	枕头套
pilose antler	lùróng	鹿茸
pilot (airplane)	fēixíngyuán	飞行员
pin (straight pin)	dàtóuzhēn	大头针
pine (tree)	sōngshù	松树
pineapple	bōluó	菠萝
ping-pong	pīngpāngqiú	乒乓球
Pingju Opera	píngjù	评剧
pink	fěnsè	粉色
pint	pǐntuō	品脱
place (n)	dìfang	地方
place of interest	kěkànde dìfang	可看的地方
plains	píngyuán	平原
plan	jìhuà, dǎsuàn	计划，打算
plane	fēijī	飞机
plant (botanical)	zhíwù	植物
plaster (medicated)	gāoyào	膏药
plate (dish)	pánzi	盘子
plateau	gāoyuán	高原
platform	píngtái	平台
platform(train station)	yuètái	月台
play (a game)	wán	玩
play (sports: hit)	dǎ	打
play (sports: kick)	tī	踢
play (theater)	huàjù	话剧
player (in a game)	xuǎnshǒu	选手
player (sports team)	duìyuán	队员
playground	cāochǎng	操场
playwright	jùzuòjiā	剧作家
please...	qǐng	请……
pleased	hěngāoxìng	很高兴
pliers	qiánzi	钳子
plot (story)	qíngjié	情节

DICTIONARY

plug (n)	chātóu	插头
plum	lǐzi	李子
plum blossom	méihuā	梅花
pneumonia	fèiyán	肺炎
poached egg	wòjīdàn,	卧鸡蛋，
	shuǐzhǔhébāodàn	水煮荷包蛋
pocket	dōu, kǒudài	兜，口袋
pocket-size	xiùzhēn	袖珍
poet	shīrén	诗人
poetry	shī	诗
poker (game)	púkè	扑克
Polaroid camera	yícì chéngxiàngjī	一次成相机
Polaroid film	pāilìdé xiàngzhǐ	拍立得相纸
police	jǐngchá	警察
police station	pàichūsuǒ	派出所
policy	zhèngcè	政策
polite	yǒulǐmào	有礼貌
political bureau	zhèngzhìjú	政治局
politics	zhèngzhì	政治
polo	mǎqiú	马球
polyester (fiber)	qínglún	晴纶
pomegranate	shíliu	石榴
pomelo (grapefruit)	yòuzi	柚子
poor (not good)	bùhǎo	不好
poor (not rich)	qióng	穷
popular music	liúxíngyīnyuè	流行音乐
porcelain	cíqì	瓷器
pork	zhūròu	猪肉
pork chop	zhūpái	猪排
porridge	zhōu	粥
port city	gǎngkǒu chéngshì	港口城市
portable	biànxiéshì	便携式
porter	xínglǐyuán	行李员
portrait	xiāoxiàng	肖像
portray	sùzào	塑造
possibility	kěnéngxíng	可能性
possible	kěnéng	可能
post (to mail)	jì	寄
post office	yóujú	邮局
postcard	míngxìnpiàn	明信片
post code (mail code)	yóuzhèng biānmǎ	邮政编码
poster	zhāotiēhuà	招贴画

pot (pan)	guō	锅
Potala Palace	bùdálā gōng	布达拉宫
potato	tǔdòu	土豆
pottery	táoqì	陶器
pound (weight)	bàng	磅
pound sterling	yīngbàng	英镑
powder	fěnmò	粉末
power (authority)	quánlì	权力
power (energy)	néngyuán	能源
power (force)	lìliàng	力量
practical (realistic)	shíjìde	实际的
practical (useful)	shíyòngde	实用的
practice (v)	liànxí	练习
prawn	dàxiā	大虾
pray	qǐdǎo	祈祷
prefer	gèng xǐhuan	更喜欢
pregnant	huáiyùn	怀孕
premenstrual tension	jīngqián jǐnzhāng	经前紧张
premier	zǒnglǐ	总理
prepare	zhǔnběi	准备
prescription	yàofāng	药方
present (current)	mùqián	目前
president (corporate)	zǒngcái	总裁
president (national)	zǒngtǒng	总统
press (clothing)	tàng	烫
press (push down)	àn	按
pretty	piàoliang	漂亮
pride	zìháo, jiāoào	自豪，骄傲
principal (school)	xiàozhǎng	校长
print (art)	bǎnhuà	版画
print (photo)	xiàngpiàn	相片
print (v)	yìn	印
printed matter	yìnshuāpǐn	印刷品
private	sīrénde	私人的
probably	dàgài	大概
problem	wèntí	问题
process (n)	guòchéng	过程
producer	shēngchǎnzhě	生产者
product	chǎnpǐn	产品
production	shēngchǎn	生产
profession	zhíyè, hángyè	职业，行业
professor	jiàoshòu	教授

DICTIONARY

program (event)	*jiémù*	节目
program (theater handout)	*jiémù dān*	节目单
prohibit	*jìnzhǐ*	禁止
promise (n)	*nuòyán*	诺言
promise (v)	*dāyìng*	答应
prop (stage accessory)	*dàojù*	道具
province	*shěng*	省
provincial museum	*shěng bówùguǎn*	省博物馆
prune	*lǐzifǔ*	李子脯
psychiatrist	*jīngshénbìng yīshēng*	精神病医生
psychologist	*xīnlǐxuéjiā*	心理学家
psychology	*xīnlǐxué*	心理学
psychosis	*jīngshénbìng*	精神病
pub	*jiǔguǎn*	酒馆
public	*gōnggòng*	公共
Public Security Bureau	*gōng ānjú*	公安局
public bus	*gōnggòng qìchē*	公共汽车
public relations	*gōnggòng guānxì*	公共关系
public square	*guǎngchǎng*	广场
Puer tea	*pǔěr chá*	普洱茶
pull	*lā*	拉
pullover	*tàotóu shān*	套头衫
pulse	*màibó*	脉搏
puncture (flat tire)	*lúntāidòng*	轮胎洞
punk	*péngkè*	朋客
puppet show	*mù ǒu xì*	木偶戏
pure	*chún*	纯
purple	*zǐsè*	紫色
purpose	*mùdì*	目的
purse	*qiánbāo*	钱包
push	*tuī*	推
put	*fàng*	放
put away (in place)	*fànghǎo*	放好
quail	*ānchún*	鹌鹑
quality	*zhìliàng*	质量
quantity	*shùliàng*	数量
quarantine	*jiǎnyì*	检疫
quart	*kuātuō*	夸脱
quarter (one-fourth)	*sìfēn zhīyī*	四分之一
quarter hour	*kè, kèzhōng*	刻，刻钟
quartet	*sìchóngzòu*	四重奏

question (n)	*wèntí*	问题
question (v)	*tíwèn*	提问
quick	*kuài*	快
quiet	*ānjìng*	安静
quilt	*bèizi*	被子
quinine	*kuíníng*	奎宁
quite	*xiāngdāng*	相当
quota	*dìng'é*	定额
rabbit	*tùzi*	兔子
racket (paddle)	*qiúpāi*	球拍
radiator	*nuǎnqì*	暖气
radio (broadcast)	*guǎngbō*	广播
radio (machine)	*shōuyīnjī*	收音机
radio program	*guǎngbō jiémù*	广播节目
radiologist	*fàngshèkē yīshī*	放射科医师
radish	*xiǎo luóbo*	小萝卜
railroad	*tiělù*	铁路
railway station	*huǒchēzhàn*	火车站
rain (n)	*yǔ*	雨
rain (v)	*xiàyǔ*	下雨
rain poncho	*yǔpī*	雨披
rainbow	*cǎihóng*	彩虹
raincoat	*yǔyī*	雨衣
raise (lift up)	*tái qǐlai*	抬起来
raisin	*pútáo gān*	葡萄干
ram	*yáng, shānyáng*	羊，山羊
ramie	*zhùmá*	苎麻
rape (vegetable)	*yóucài*	油菜
rape (assault)	*qiángjiān*	强奸
rash (on skin)	*pízhěn*	皮疹
rat	*lǎoshǔ*	老鼠
rate (price)	*jiàgé*	价格
rather (prefer to)	*nìngyuàn*	宁愿
ratio	*bǐlì*	比例
ravioli	*jiǎozi*	饺子
(boiled dumplings)		
rayon	*rénzào sī*	人造丝
razor	*tìdāo, guāhúdāo*	剃刀，刮胡刀
razor blade	*dāopiàn*	刀片
read	*dú, kàn*	读，看
read aloud	*niàn*	念

DICTIONARY

read books	*kàn shū*	看书
real	*zhēn*	真
real estate agent	*dìchǎn jīngjìrén*	地产经纪人
really	*zhēnde*	真的
reason (cause)	*yuányīn*	原因
reason (logic)	*dàoli*	道理
receipt (sales slip)	*fāpiào*	发票
receive (goods)	*shōu*	收
recently	*jìnlái*	近来
reception	*jiēdài*	接待
reception desk	*jiēdài chù*	接待处
reception personnel	*jiēdài rényuán*	接待人员
reception room	*jiēdài shì*	接待室
recipe (cooking)	*shípǔ*	食谱
recipient	*shōujiànrén, duìfāng*	收件人，对方
recite	*bèi*	背
recommend	*tuījiàn*	推荐
record store	*chàngpiāndiàn*	唱片店
recreation room	*yùlè shì*	娱乐室
red	*hóng*	红
red-crowned crane	*dāndǐnghè*	丹顶鹤
red paste (for seals)	*yìnní*	印泥
red wine	*hóngjiǔ*	红酒
reference (for study)	*cānkǎo*	参考
reform	*gǎigé*	改革
refreshment (cold drinks)	*lěngyǐn*	冷饮
refreshment (snacks)	*xiǎochī*	小吃
refreshment stand	*xiǎochī tān*	小吃摊
refrigerator	*bīngxiāng*	冰箱
refund	*chánghuái*	偿还
region	*dìqū*	地区
register	*dēngjì*	登记
registered (mail)	*guàhào*	挂号
registration desk	*dēngjì chù*	登记处
registration office (hospital)	*guàhào chù*	挂号处
regret	*hòuhuǐ*	后悔
regulation	*guīdìng*	规定
rehearsal	*páiliàn*	排练
relative (kin)	*qīnqī*	亲戚
relatives (kinfolk)	*qīnshǔ*	亲属
relevance	*guānxi*	关系

relief (sculpture)	*fúdiāo*	浮雕
remain (stay)	*liú*	留
remember	*jìde*	记得
Renault	*léinuò*	雷诺
rent (v)	*zū*	租
rental fee	*zūjīn*	租金
repair	*xiūlǐ*	修理
repeat	*chóngfù*	重复
reprint (v)	*jiāyìn*	加印
reproduction (replica)	*fùzhìpǐn*	复制品
request	*yāoqiú*	要求
reroute	*gǎihuàn*	改换
research institute	*yánjiūsuǒ*	研究所
resemble	*xiàng*	像
reservations desk	*yùdìng chù*	预订处
reserve (v)	*yùdìng*	预订
reside	*zhù*	住
residence permit	*jūliú zhèng*	居留证
respect	*zūnjìng*	尊敬
rest (relax)	*xiūxi*	休息
restaurant	*fànguǎn, cāntīng*	饭馆，餐厅
result	*jiéguǒ*	结果
retail	*língshòu*	零售
retired worker	*tuìxiū gōngrén*	退休工人
return (come back)	*huí*	回
return (give back)	*huán*	还
return (merchandise)	*tuì*	退
reunion	*tuánjù*	团聚
review (critique)	*pínglùn*	评论
review (study again)	*fùxí*	复习
revolution	*gémìng*	革命
rheumatism	*fēngshī bìng*	风湿病
rib (n)	*lèigǔ*	肋骨
rice (cooked)	*mǐfàn*	米饭
rice (crop)	*dàozi*	稻子
rice porridge (congee)	*xīfàn, zhōu*	稀饭,粥
rich (prosperous)	*fù*	富
ride (a bicycle)	*qí*	骑
ride (a car)	*zuò*	坐
ride (an animal)	*qí*	骑
right (correct)	*duì*	对
right (direction)	*yòu*	右

DICTIONARY

right away	mǎshàng	马上
ring (jewelry)	jièzhi	戒指
ring road (as part of a street)	huán	环
riot	bàoluàn	暴乱
rise (go up, increase)	shàngshēng	上升
river	hé, jiāng	河，江
road	lù, mǎlù	路，马路
roadside	lùbiān	路边
roast (v)	kǎo	烤
roast pork bun	chāshāo bāo	叉烧包
roast suckling pig	kǎorǔzhū	烤乳猪
rock-and-roll	yáogǔn yuè	摇滚乐
rock climbing	pānyán	攀岩
roll (n)	juǎn	卷
Rome	luómǎ	罗马
roof	fángdǐng	房顶
room (in a building)	fángjiān	房间
room number	fánghào	房号
roommate	tóngwū	同屋
rooster	gōngjī	公鸡
rope	shéngzi	绳子
rope skipping (Chinese)	tiào píjīn	跳皮筋
rose (flower)	méiguìhuā	玫瑰花
rose, Chinese	yuèjì	月季
rough	cūcāo	粗糙
round (shape)	yuán	圆
round-trip ticket	láihuí piào	来回票
route	lù	路
row (column, line)	pái	排
rowboat	xiǎochuán	小船
rowing (sport)	huátǐng	划艇
rubbing alcohol	yīyòng jiǔjīng	医用酒精
rude	cūbào	粗暴
rug	dìtǎn	地毯
ruins	yízhǐ	遗址
ruler (measuring) (stick)	chǐzi	尺子
runny nose	liú bíti	流鼻涕
rural	nóngcūn	农村
rush service	jiājí fúwù	加急服务
Russian (language)	éyǔ	俄语
rusty	xiù le	锈了

sable	zǐdiāo	紫貂
Sacred Way	shéndào	神道
safety pin	biézhēn	别针
salad	shālā	沙拉
salary	gōngzī	工资
sales counter	shòuhuòtái, guìtái	售货台，柜台
sales manager	xiāoshòu jīnglǐ	销售经理
salesperson	tuīxiāoyuán	推销员
saline solution	shēnglǐ yánshuǐ	生理盐水
saliva	kǒushuǐ	口水
salt	yán	盐
salted duck egg	xián yādàn	咸鸭蛋
salty	xián	咸
same	yíyàng	一样
sample good	yàngpǐn	样品
San Francisco	jiùjīnshān	旧金山
sand	shāzi	沙子
sandals	liángxié	凉鞋
sandalwood fan	tánxiāng shàn	檀香扇
sandwich	sānmíngzhì	三明治
sanitary napkin	wèishēng jīn	卫生巾
Santana	sāngtǎnà	桑塔纳
satellite	wèixīng	卫星
satisfied	mǎnyìde	满意的
satisfy	mǎnzú	满足
Saturday	xīngqī liù	星期六
sauce	jiàng	酱
sausage	xiāngcháng	香肠
sautéed	chǎo	炒
say	shuō	说
scallion	cōng	葱
scallop	gānbèi	干贝
scarf	wéijīn	围巾
scarlet fever	xīnghóngrè	猩红热
scenery	fēngjǐng	风景
schedule (timetable)	shíkè biǎo	时刻表
schizophrenia	jīngshén fēnliè zhèng	精神分裂症
school	xuéxiào	学校
school (of thought)	liúpài	流派
science	kēxué	科学
scientist	kēxuéjiā	科学家

DICTIONARY

scissors	*jiǎndāo*	剪刀
scrambled eggs	*chǎo jīdàn*	炒鸡蛋
screen (n)	*píngfēng*	屏风
screw (n)	*luósīdīng*	螺丝钉
screwdriver	*luósīdāo*	螺丝刀
script (play or film)	*jiǎoběn*	脚本
sculptor	*diāosù jiā*	雕塑家
sculpture	*diāosù*	雕塑
sea	*hǎi*	海
sea cucumber	*hǎishēn*	海参
seafood	*hǎixiān*	海鲜
season (n)	*jìjié*	季节
seat (n)	*zuòwèi*	座位
seat number	*zuòhào*	座号
seatbelt	*ānquándài*	安全带
second (fraction of time)	*miǎo*	秒
secret	*mìmì*	秘密
secretariat	*shūjìchù*	书记处
secretary, office	*mìshū*	秘书
security guard	*ānquán rényuán*	安全人员
see	*kànjiàn*	看见
see off	*sòng*	送
See you later.	*huítóujiàn*	回头见。
seem	*hǎoxiàng*	好像
self	*zìjǐ, zìgěr*	自己，自个儿
self-portrait	*zìhuàxiàng*	自画像
self-timer (camera)	*zìpāi*	自拍
sell	*mài*	卖
seminar	*yántǎohuì*	研讨会
send a telegram	*fā diànbào*	发电报
send an email	*fā diànzǐyóujiàn*	发电子邮件
senior citizen	*lǎoniánrén*	老年人
sentence (n)	*jùzi*	句子
Seoul	*shǒuěr*	首尔
September	*jiǔyuè*	九月
serious (earnest)	*rènzhēn*	认真
serious (grave)	*yánzhòng*	严重
servant	*púrén*	仆人
service	*fúwù*	服务
service attendant	*fúwùyuán*	服务员
service desk	*fúwùtái*	服务台
service fee	*fúwùfèi*	服务费

service, religious	*lǐbài*	礼拜
sesame biscuit	*shāobǐng*	烧饼
sesame oil	*máyóu*	麻油
set (matching pieces)	*tào*	套
set (theater)	*bùjǐng*	布景
set design	*bùjǐng shèjì*	布景设计
settle (pay) the bill	*jiézhàng*	结账
seven	*qī*	七
seventy	*qīshí*	七十
several	*hǎo jǐgè*	好几个
sew	*féng*	缝
sex	*xìng*	性
shadow	*yǐng*	影
shadow puppet	*píyǐng*	皮影
shake hands	*wòshǒu*	握手
shampoo	*xiāngbō*	香波
Shanghai Opera	*hùjù*	沪剧
Shangri-La	*xiānggélǐlā*	香格里拉
Shaoxing Opera	*yuèjù, shàoxīng xì*	越剧,绍兴戏
Shaoxing rice wine	*shàoxīng jiāfàn jiǔ*	绍兴加饭酒
share (an expense)	*fēntān*	分摊
shark's fin soup	*yúchì tāng*	鱼翅汤
sharp (edge)	*fēnglì*	锋利
shattered	*suìle*	碎了
shave	*guāliǎn*	刮脸
shaver, electric	*diàn tìdāo*	电剃刀
she	*tā*	她
sheep	*yáng*	羊
sheet (of paper)	*zhāng*	张
sheets (linen)	*chuángdān*	床单
shelf	*jiàzi*	架子
shell mosaic	*bèidiāochù*	贝雕画
Sheraton	*xǐláidēng*	喜来登
shiny	*shǎnguāng*	闪光
ship (n)	*chuán*	船
ship (v)	*hǎiyùn*	海运
shipping company	*hángyùn gōngsī*	航运公司
shirt	*chènshān*	衬衫
shiver	*fādǒu*	发抖
shock (n)	*xiūkè*	休克
shoe	*xié*	鞋
shoe polish	*xiéyóu*	鞋油

DICTIONARY

shoehorn	xiébázi	鞋拔子
shoelace	xiédài	鞋带
shooting (sport)	shèjī	射击
shop (n)	shāngdiàn, pùzi	商店，铺子
shopping	mǎi dōngxi	买东西
short (height)	ǎi	矮
short (length)	duǎn	短
should	yīnggāi	应该
shoulder (n)	jiānbǎng	肩膀
shoulder bag	bēibāo	背包
show (performance)	biǎoyǎn, yǎnchū	表演，演出
show (to demonstrate)	shìfàn	示范
shower	línyù	淋浴
shower cap	línyù mào	淋浴帽
shredded dried meat	ròusōng	肉松
shrimp	xiā	虾
shrine	jìtán	祭坛
shut	guān, bì	关，闭
shutter (camera)	kuàimén	快门
Siberia	xībólìyà	西伯利亚
sickness	bìng	病
side (body)	cèlèi	侧肋
side (margin)	biān	边
sidewalk	rénxíngdào	人行道
sightsee	guānguāng, yóulǎn	观光，游览
sign (notice board)	báizi	牌子
sign (symbol)	biāojì	标记
signature	qiānmíng	签名
silent	wúshēng	无声
silk (pure)	zhēnsī	真丝
silk and brocade factory	sīzhī chǎng	丝织厂
silk cocoon factory	sāosī chǎng	缫丝厂
silk fabric	sīchóu	丝绸
silk mill	sīchóu chǎng	丝绸厂
silk products shop	sīchóu shāngdiàn	丝绸商店
Silk Road	sīchóu zhīlù	丝绸之路
silkworm	cán	蚕
silver	yín	银
simulate	mónǐ	模拟
sing	chànggē	唱歌
Singapore	xīnjiāpō	新加坡

160

singer	gēchàng jiā, gēshǒu	歌唱家,歌手
single room	dānjiān	单间
sink	shuǐchízi	水池子
sister (older)	jiějie	姐姐
sister (younger)	mèimei	妹妹
sit	zuò	坐
six	liù	六
sixty	liùshí	六十
size (measurement)	chǐcùn, guīgé	尺寸,规格
size (number)	hào	号
sketch (art)	sùxiě	速写
sketch (design draft)	cǎotú	草图
skiing	huáxuě	滑雪
skill	jìqiǎo	技巧
skin	pífū	皮肤
skirt	qúnzi	裙子
sky	tiānkōng	天空
sky-diving	tiàosǎn	跳伞
sleep (v)	shuìjiào	睡觉
sleeping bag	shuìdài	睡袋
sleeping pill	ānmián yào	安眠药
slice (n)	piàn	片
slide (photo)	huàndēng piàn	幻灯片
slide film	fǎnzhuǎn piàn	反转片
slide mount	huàndēngpiàn kuàng	幻灯片框
slip (petticoat)	chènqún	衬裙
slippers	tuōxié	拖鞋
slow	màn	慢
small	xiǎo	小
smell (n)	wèidao, wèi	味道,味
smell (v)	wén	闻
smile	wēixiào	微笑
smoke cigarettes	chōuyān	抽烟
smoked fish	xūnyú	熏鱼
snack	xiǎochī, diǎnxin	小吃,点心
snake	shé	蛇
snow (n)	xuě	雪
snow (v)	xiàxuě	下雪
snow mountain	xuěshān	雪山
snow peas	xuědòu	雪豆
snuff bottle	bíyānhú	鼻烟壶
snuff box	bíyānhé	鼻烟盒

DICTIONARY

so (therefore)	suǒyǐ	所以
so-so	yìbān, mǎmǎhūhū	一般，马马虎虎
soap (n)	féizào	肥皂
soccer	zúqiú	足球
soccer match	zúqiú bǐsài	足球比赛
social dancing	jiāojì wǔ	交际舞
sociology	shèhuìxué	社会学
socket (electrical)	chāzuò	插座
socks	wàzi	袜子
soda pop	qìshuǐ	汽水
soda water	sūdá shuǐ	苏打水
sofa	shāfā	沙发
soft-seat	ruǎnxí	软席
soft-sleeper	ruǎnwò	软卧
softball	lěiqiú	垒球
soil (n)	tǔ, tǔrǎng	土，土壤
soldier	shìbīng, jūnrén	士兵，军人
solo (dance)	dúwǔ	独舞
solo (instrumental)	dúzòu	独奏
solo (vocal)	dúchàng	独唱
solution (method)	bànfǎ	办法
solve	jiějué	解决
some	yìxiē	一些
sometimes	yǒushí	有时
son	érzi	儿子
sonata	zòumíngqǔ	奏鸣曲
song	gēqǔ	歌曲
song-and-dance	gēwǔ	歌舞
song-and-dance troupe	gēwǔ tuán	歌舞团
Sony	suǒní	索尼
soon	mǎshàng, yíhuìr	马上，一会儿
sore (ache)	suānténgde, téngde	酸疼的，疼的
sore throat	hóulóng téng	喉咙疼
soreness	téngtòng	疼痛
sorghum	gāoliáng	高粱
sound (n)	shēngyīn	声音
sound effect	yīnxiào	音效
soup	tāng	汤
soup noodles	tāngmiàn	汤面
sour	suānde	酸的
south	nán	南
South America	nánměizhōu	南美洲

South China Sea	*nánhǎi*	南海
Soviet Union	*sūlián*	(前) 苏联
soy sauce	*jiàngyóu*	酱油
soybean	*huángdòu*	黄豆
soybean milk	*dòujiāng*	豆浆
space	*kōngjiān*	空间
space shuttle	*hángtiān fēijī*	航天飞机
spare time	*yèyú shíjiān*	业余时间
sparerib	*páigǔ*	排骨
speak	*jiǎng*	讲
special delivery (mail)	*kuàidì*	快递
speed limit	*xiàn sù*	限速
spend	*huā*	花
spicy (hot)	*là*	辣
spinach	*bōcài*	菠菜
spine	*jǐzhuī*	脊椎
splinter (n)	*cì*	刺
spoke (wheel)	*chētiáo*	车条
spoon	*sháozi*	勺子
sporting goods	*tǐyù yòngpǐn*	体育用品
sports	*yùndòng*	运动
sports event	*yùndòng xiàngmù*	运动项目
spotlight	*jùguāngdēng*	聚光灯
spouse	*pèiǒu*	配偶
sprained	*niǔshāng*	扭伤
spring (season)	*chūntiān*	春天
spring roll	*chūnjuǎn*	春卷
square (area measure)	*píngfāng*	平方
square (shape)	*fāng*	方
square meter	*píngfāng mǐ*	平方米
squid	*yóuyú*	鱿鱼
stadium	*tǐyùchǎng*	体育场
stage (n)	*wǔtái*	舞台
stage (of progress)	*jiēduàn*	阶段
stainless steel	*búxiùgāng*	不锈钢
stairs	*lóutī*	楼梯
stale	*bù xīnxiān*	不新鲜
stamp (postage)	*yóupiào*	邮票
stamp collecting	*jíyóu*	集邮
stand (n)	*jiàzi*	架子
stand (v)	*zhàn*	站
standard	*biāozhǔn*	标准

DICTIONARY

standing committee	*chángwù wěiyuánhuì*	常务委员会
star (celebrity)	*míngxīng*	明星
star (n)	*xīngxing*	星星
Starbucks	*xīngbākè*	星巴克
state council	*guówùyuàn*	国务院
station (depot)	*zhàn*	站
stationary	*jìngzhǐde, wěndìngde*	静止的，稳定的
stationery (writing paper)	*xìnzhǐ*	信纸
statue	*sùxiàng, diāoxiàng*	塑像，雕像
stay (live, spend time)	*dāi*	呆
steak (beef)	*niúpái*	牛排
steam (v)	*zhēng*	蒸
steamed bun	*mántou*	馒头
steamed dumpling	*bāozi*	包子
steamed twisted roll	*huājuǎn*	花卷
steel	*gāng*	钢
steep (in hot water)	*pào*	泡
steep (hill)	*dǒu*	陡
steering wheel	*fāngxiàngpái*	方向盘
stele	*shíbǎn, shízhù*	石板，石柱
step (footstep)	*bù*	步
stereo system	*zǔhé yīnxiǎng*	组合音响
stew (v)	*dùn*	炖
stiff	*jiāngyìngde*	僵硬的
still (further)	*hái*	还
still (motionless)	*bú dòng, tíngzhǐ*	不动，停止
still (yet)	*yīrán, réngrán*	依然，仍然
still life painting	*jìngwù huà*	静物画
stir-fry	*chǎo*	炒
Stockholm	*sīdégēěrmó*	斯德哥尔摩
stockings	*chángtǒng wà*	长筒袜
stocks (shares)	*gǔpiào*	股票
stomach	*wèi, dùzi*	胃，肚子
stomachache	*wèiténg*	胃疼
stone (n)	*shítou*	石头
Stone Forest	*shílín*	石林
stone rubbing	*tàpiàn*	拓片
stop (station)	*zhàn*	站
stop (v)	*tíng*	停
store (put away)	*cúnfàng*	存放
store (shop)	*diàn, shāngdiàn*	店，商店
storyteller	*shuōshū rén*	说书人

storytelling	*shuōshū*	说书
straight	*zhí*	直
straits (waterway)	*hǎixiá*	海峡
strange	*qíguài*	奇怪
stranger (person)	*mòshēng rén*	陌生人
strawberry	*cǎoméi*	草莓
street	*jiē*	街
strength	*lìliang, lìqi*	力量，力气
strict	*yán*	严
string (n)	*shéngzi*	绳子
string bean	*sìjìdòu*	四季豆
string instrument	*xián yuèqì*	弦乐器
string quartet	*xiányuè sìchóngzòu*	弦乐四重奏
striped	*yǒu tiáowén de*	有条纹的
stroke (paralysis)	*zhòngfēng*	中风
strong	*qiángliè*	强烈
struggle	*dòuzhēng*	斗争
stuck	*dǔzhù le*	堵住了
student	*xuéshēng*	学生
study (v)	*xué*	学
study abroad	*liúxué*	留学
stuffy (unventilated)	*mēn*	闷
stupid	*bèn, chǔn*	笨，蠢
sturdy	*jiēshi*	结实
style	*fēnggé*	风格
suburb	*jiāoqū*	郊区
subway	*dìtiě*	地铁
subway station	*dìtiě chēzhàn*	地铁车站
success	*chénggōng*	成功
sugar	*táng*	糖
sugar cane	*gānzhe*	甘蔗
suit (clothing)	*xīzhuāng*	西装
suitcase	*xiāngzi*	箱子
suite (room)	*tàojiān*	套间
sulfa	*huáng ān*	磺胺
summer	*xiàtiān*	夏天
Summer Palace	*yíhéyuán*	颐和园
sun	*tàiyáng*	太阳
Sun Yat-sen	*sūn zhōngshān*	孙中山
sunburn	*shàishāng*	晒伤
Sunday	*xīngqī rì*	星期日
sunglasses	*mòjìng*	墨镜

DICTIONARY

sunlight	*yángguāng*	阳光
sunrise	*rìchū*	日出
sunscreen	*fángshàishuāng*	防晒霜
sunset	*rìluò*	日落
sunstroke	*zhòngshǔ*	中暑
supervisor	*jiāndū rén*	监督人
support (an endeavor)	*zhīchí*	支持
surface mail	*píngxìn*	平信
surgeon	*wàikē yīshēng*	外科医生
surgery	*shǒushù*	手术
surgery department	*wàikē*	外科
surprised	*jīngya*	惊讶
sutra	*fójīng*	佛经
swallow (v)	*yàn*	咽
sweat (n)	*hàn*	汗
sweat (v)	*chūhàn*	出汗
sweater	*máoyī*	毛衣
sweatpants	*yùndòng chángkù*	运动长裤
sweatshirt	*chángxiù yùndòngshān*	长袖运动衫
Sweden	*ruìdiǎn*	瑞典
sweep	*sǎo*	扫
sweet	*tián*	甜
sweet-and-sour	*tángcù*	糖醋
sweet-and-sour pork	*gǔlǎo ròu*	古老肉
sweet potato	*báishǔ, hóngshǔ*	白薯，红薯
swelling	*zhǒngzhàng*	肿胀
swim	*yóuyǒng*	游泳
swimming pool	*yóuyǒngchí*	游泳池
swimsuit	*yóuyǒngyī*	游泳衣
swing (playground)	*qiūqiān*	秋千
switchboard	*zǒngjī*	总机
Switzerland	*ruìshì*	瑞士
sword bean	*dāodòu*	刀豆
Sydney	*xīní*	悉尼
symbol	*biāozhì*	标志
symbolize	*xiàngzhēng*	象征
sympathetic	*tóngqíngde*	同情的
symphony	*jiāoxiǎng yuè*	交响乐
symphony orchestra	*jiāoxiǎng yuèduì*	交响乐队
symptom	*zhèngzhuàng*	症状
synthetic (fiber)	*huàxiān*	化纤
syrup	*tángjiāng*	糖浆

system	*xìtǒng*	系统
T-intersection	*dīngzì lùkǒu*	丁字路口
T-shirt	*duǎnxiù shān*	短袖衫
table (n)	*zhuōzi*	桌子
tablecloth	*táibù, zhuōbù*	台布，桌布
tablespoon	*tāngsháo*	汤勺
tablet	*yàopiàn*	药片
taillight	*wěidēng*	尾灯
tailor (n)	*cáifeng*	裁缝
Taipei	*táiběi*	台北
Taiwan	*táiwān*	台湾
take (hold)	*ná*	拿
take (medication)	*fúyào*	服药
take a picture	*zhào zhāng xiàng*	照张相
take away	*názǒu*	拿走
take interest in	*duì...gǎn xìngqù*	对……感兴趣
take off (flights)	*qǐfēi*	起飞
talk (converse)	*tánhuà, jiāotán*	谈话，交谈
tamer	*xùnshòu yuán*	驯兽员
tampon	*wèishēng miántiáo*	卫生棉条
Tang figurine (tri-colored)	*tángsāncǎi*	唐三彩
tangerine	*júzi*	橘子
tango	*tàngē*	探戈
Taoism	*dàojiào*	道教
tap (faucet)	*shuǐlóngtóu*	水龙头
tape (cellophane)	*tòumíng jiāodài*	透明胶带
tape (sound)	*lùyīncídài*	录音磁带
tape measure	*juǎnchǐ*	卷尺
tape recorder	*lùyīnjī*	录音机
tapestry	*bìtǎn*	壁毯
taro	*yùtou*	芋头
taste (n)	*wèidào*	味道
taste (v)	*cháng*	尝
tax (n)	*shuì*	税
taxi (n)	*chūzū qìchē*	出租汽车
tea	*chá*	茶
tea plantation (factory)	*cháchǎng*	茶厂
tea set	*chájù*	茶具
tea shop	*cháye diàn*	茶叶店
teach	*jiāo*	教
teacher	*lǎoshī, jiàoshī*	老师，教师

DICTIONARY

teacup	chábēi	茶杯
teapot	cháhú	茶壶
teaspoon	xiǎochí, cháchí	小匙,茶匙
technician	jìshùyuán	技术员
teeth	yáchǐ	牙齿
telegram	diànbào	电报
telephone (n)	diànhuà	电话
telephone (v)	dǎ diànhuà	打电话
telephone number	diànhuà hàomǎ	电话号码
television	diànshì	电视
television set	diànshìjī	电视机
television station	diànshìtái	电视台
telex	diànchuán	电传
telex machine	diànchuánjī	电传机
tell	gàosù	告诉
temperature (general)	wēndù	温度
temperature (of body)	tǐwēn	体温
temple (Buddhist)	sì, miào	寺,庙
temple (Taoist)	guàn	观
Temple of Heaven	tiāntán	天坛
ten	shí	十
tent	zhàngpéng	帐篷
ten thousand	wàn	万
tendon	jīn	筋
tennis	wǎngqiú	网球
terracotta figure	bīngmǎyǒng	兵马俑
terrible	kěpà, zāogāo	可怕, 糟糕
test (exam)	kǎoshì	考试
tetanus	pòshāngfēng	破伤风
text message (communication)	duǎnxìn	短信
textile	fǎngzhīpǐn	纺织品
Thailand	tàiguó	泰国
thank you	xièxie	谢谢
that	nà	那
that one	nàge, nèige	那个
theater	jùchǎng	剧场
theater troupe	jùtuán	剧团
their	tāmende	他们的
them	tāmen	他们
there	nàli, nàr	那里，那儿
therefore	yīncǐ	因此

thermal pants	*miānmáo kù*	棉毛裤
thermal shirt	*miānmáo shān*	棉毛衫
thermometer	*wēndù biǎo*	温度表
thermos	*nuǎnshuǐpíng*	暖水瓶
these	*zhèxiē*	这些
they	*tāmen*	他们
thick (coarse)	*cū*	粗
thick (dense)	*nóng*	浓
thick (layer)	*hòu*	厚
thin (layer)	*báo*	薄
thin (slender)	*shòu, xì*	瘦，细
thin (sparse)	*xī*	稀
thing	*dōngxi*	东西
think (believe)	*rènwéi*	认为
thirsty	*kě*	渴
thirty	*sānshí*	三十
this	*zhè*	这
this one	*zhège, zhèige*	这个
this year	*jīnnián*	今年
those	*nàxiē, nèixiē*	那些
thousand	*qiān*	千
thousand-year egg (preserved duck egg)	*pídàn, sōnghuādàn*	皮蛋，松花蛋
thread (n)	*xiàn*	线
three	*sān*	三
Three Gorges	*sānxiá*	三峡
three delicacies soup	*sānxiān tāng*	三鲜汤
three-dimensional	*lìtǐ*	立体
three-prong plug	*sānxiàng chātóu*	三相插头
throat	*hóulóng*	喉咙
throw	*rēng*	扔
throw away	*rēngdiào*	扔掉
thunder	*léi*	雷
Thursday	*xīngqī sì*	星期四
Tibet	*xīzàng*	西藏
ticket	*piào*	票
ticket office	*shòupiào chù*	售票处
ticket seller	*shòupiàoyuán*	售票员
tie (necktie)	*lǐngdài*	领带
tie up	*kǔn qǐlai*	捆起来
tiger	*lǎohǔ*	老虎
tiger balm	*qīngliángyóu*	清凉油

DICTIONARY

tight	jǐn	紧
tile (n)	wǎ	瓦
timber	mùliào	木料
time (n)	shíjiān	时间
time (occasion)	cì	次
time period (historic)	niándài	年代
timer	jìshí qì	计时器
timetable	shíkè biǎo	时刻表
tip (gratuity)	xiǎofèi	小费
tire (wheel)	chētāi	车胎
tire pump	qìtǒng	气筒
tired	lèi	累
tissue	zhǐjīn	纸巾
toast (bread)	kǎo miànbāo	烤面包
today	jīntiān	今天
toe	jiǎozhǐ	脚趾
toilet	cèsuǒ	厕所
toilet paper	wèishēng zhǐ	卫生纸
Tokyo	dōngjīng	东京
tomato	xīhóngshì, fānqié	西红柿，番茄
tomato sauce	fānqié jiàng	番茄酱
tomb	fénmù	坟墓
tombs, imperial	huánglíng	皇陵
tomorrow	míngtiān	明天
ton	dūn	吨
tongue	shétou	舌头
tonight	jīnwǎn	今晚
tonsils	biǎntǎoxiàn	扁桃腺
too (also)	yě	也
too (excessive)	tài	太
tool	gōngjù	工具
tooth	yá	牙
toothache	yáténg	牙疼
toothbrush	yáshuā	牙刷
toothpaste	yágāo	牙膏
toothpick	yáqiān	牙签
top (height)	dǐng	顶
torn	pòle	破了
Toronto	duōlúnduō	多伦多
tortoise	wūguī	乌龟
touch-me-not	fèngxiānhuā	凤仙花
tour escort	lǐngduì	领队

tour group	*lǚyóu tuán*	旅游团
tourist	*yóukè*	游客
tournament	*bǐsài*	比赛
toward	*wǎng, xiàng*	往，向
towel	*máojīn*	毛巾
town	*zhèn*	镇
township	*xiāng*	乡
toy	*wánjù*	玩具
toy store	*wánjù diàn*	玩具店
Toyota	*fēngtián*	丰田
track and field	*tiánjìng*	田径
tractor	*tuōlājī*	拖拉机
trade (business)	*màoyì*	贸易
traditional	*chuántǒngde*	传统的
traffic	*jiāotōng*	交通
traffic circle	*jiāotōng huándǎo*	交通环岛
traffic jam	*dǔchē*	堵车
traffic light	*hónglǜdēng*	红绿灯
tragedy	*bēijù*	悲剧
train (railroad)	*huǒchē*	火车
train station	*huǒchēzhàn*	火车站
training	*xùnliàn*	训练
tranquilizer	*zhènjìngjì*	镇静剂
transfer (bus, train)	*dǎo, huàn*	倒，换
transformer (voltage)	*biànyāqì*	变压器
transit visa	*guòjìng qiānzhèng*	过境签证
translate	*fānyì*	翻译
translator	*fānyì*	翻译
transparent	*tòumíngde*	透明的
travel	*lǚxíng*	旅行
travel permit	*lǚyóu xǔkězhèng*	旅游许可证
travel service (agency)	*lǚxíngshè*	旅行社
travel sickness	*lǚxíng xuányūn*	旅行眩晕
traveler's check	*lǚxíng zhīpiào*	旅行支票
traveling bag	*lǚxíng bāo*	旅行包
tree	*shù*	树
tribe	*bùluò, jiāzú*	部落，家族
trick (v)	*piàn*	骗
tricycle (child's)	*értóng chē*	儿童车
tricycle (pedicab)	*sānlún chē*	三轮车
trim	*xiūjiǎn*	修剪

DICTIONARY

trio (instrumental)	*sānchóngzòu*	三重奏
trip (travel)	*lǚxíng*	旅行
tripod	*sānjiǎojià*	三角架
trolley	*wúguǐ diànchē*	无轨电车
truck (n)	*kǎchē*	卡车
true	*zhēnde*	真的
trunk (car)	*xíngli xiāng*	行李箱
trunk (luggage)	*píxiāng*	皮箱
truth	*zhēnlǐ*	真理
try	*shì yíxià*	试一下
tuberculosis	*fèi jiéhé*	肺结核
Tuesday	*xīngqī èr*	星期二
tug of war	*báhé*	拔河
turn (a corner)	*guǎiwān*	拐弯
turn around (head back)	*diàotóu, huízhuǎn*	掉头，回转
turn off (to shut off)	*guān*	关
turn on (to switch on)	*kāi*	开
turnip	*luóbo*	萝卜
turtle	*wūguī*	乌龟
twenty	*èrshí*	二十
twin bed	*dānrén chuáng*	单人床
twin room	*shuāngrén fángjiān*	双人房间
two (the number)	*èr*	二
two (the quantity)	*liǎng*	两
two-prong plug (flat prongs)	*píngjiǎo chātóu*	平角插头
two-prong plug (round prongs)	*yuánjiǎo chātóu*	圆角插头
type (kind)	*zhǒnglèi*	种类
typewriter	*dǎzìjī*	打字机
typhoid	*shānghán*	伤寒
typhoon	*táifēng*	台风
typhus	*bānzhěn shānghán*	斑疹伤寒
typist	*dǎzìyuán*	打字员
ugly	*chǒu, nánkàn*	丑，难看
ulcer	*kuìyáng*	溃疡
ultrasound	*chāoshēngbō*	超声波
umbrella	*yǔsǎn*	雨伞
uncle (see Appendix H)	*shūshu*	叔叔
under	*zài...xiàmiàn*	……在下面

underground (adj)	dìxià	地下
underpass	dìxià tōngdào	地下通道
understand	dǒng	懂
underwear	nèiyī	内衣
unemployed	shīyè	失业
uniform	zhìfú	制服
unit (organization)	dānwèi	单位
united	liánhé	联合
United Nations	liánhéguó	联合国
United States	měiguó	美国
university	dàxué	大学
until	dào...wéizhǐ	到……为止
up	shàng	上
uphill	shàngshān	上山
upstairs	lóushàng	楼上
urban	chéngshì	城市
urinate	xiǎobiàn	小便
US dollar	měiyuán	美元
use (n)	yòngtú	用途
use (v)	yòng	用
useful	yǒu yòngde	有用的
usually	tōngcháng, jīngcháng	通常，经常
vacation (n)	jiàjī, jià	假期，假
vacation, spend a	dùjià	度假
vaccination certificate	fángyìzhèng	防疫证
vacuum cleaner	xīchénqì	吸尘器
vague	mōhude	模糊的
valley	shāngǔ	山谷
valuable object	guìzhòng wùpǐn	贵重物品
value (n)	jiàzhí	价值
van (mini-bus)	miànbāochē	面包车
Vancouver	wēngēhuá	温哥华
vase	huāpíng	花瓶
vegetable	shūcài	蔬菜
vegetarian food	sùshí	素食
vein (blood)	jìngmài	静脉
venereal disease	xìngbìng	性病
ventilation	tōngfēng	通风
vermicelli (dried)	guàmiàn	挂面
vertical flute (bamboo)	xiāo	箫
very	hěn	很

DICTIONARY

vest	bèixīn	背心
vice-president (national)	fù zǒngtǒng	副总统
video camera	shèxiàng jī	摄像机
video cassette recorder	lùxiàng jī	录像机
videotape	lùxiàngdài	录像带
Vietnam	yuènán	越南
view (scenery)	jǐngsè	景色
viewfinder	qǔjǐngqì	取景器
village	cūnzhuāng	村庄
village fair	jíshì	集市
villain	ègùn	恶棍
vinegar	cù	醋
violin	xiǎotíqín	小提琴
visa	qiānzhèng	签证
visa office (PSB)	gōng ānjú wàiguǎnchù	公安局外管处
visit	cānguān, fǎngwèn	参观,访问
visit relatives	tànqīn	探亲
vocabulary	cíhuì liàng	词汇量
vodka	fútèjiā	伏特加
voice (n)	sǎngzi	嗓子
volleyball	páiqiú	排球
voltage	diànyā	电压
voltage converter	biànyāqì	变压器
volts, 110	yìbǎi yīshí fú	110伏
volts, 220	èrbǎi èrshí fú	220伏
volume (book)	juàn	卷
volume (sound)	yīnliàng	音量
vomit	ǒutù	呕吐
wage (salary)	gōngzī	工资
waist	yāo	腰
waist drum	yāogǔ	腰鼓
wait	děng	等
waiter or waitress	fúwùyuán	服务员
waiting lounge	hòukèshì	候客室
wake up (self)	xǐnglái	醒来
wake up (someone else)	jiàoxǐng	叫醒
walk	zǒu, sànbù	走,散步
Walkman (personal stereo)	dānfàngjī, suíshēntīng	单放机,随身听
wall	qiáng	墙
wallet	píjiāzi	皮夹子

walnut	*hétao*	核桃
waltz (dance)	*huá ěrzi*	华尔兹
waltz (music)	*yuánwǔqǔ*	圆舞曲
want (v)	*yào*	要
war	*zhànzhēng*	战争
warm (adj)	*nuǎnhe*	暖和
warm (personality)	*rèqíng*	热情
wash (v)	*xǐ*	洗
washcloth	*xǐliǎn jīn*	洗脸巾
Washington DC	*huáshèngdùn tèqū*	华盛顿特区
waste (v)	*làngfèi*	浪费
wastebasket	*zhǐlǒu*	纸篓
watch (v)	*kàn*	看
watch (wristwatch)	*shǒubiǎo*	手表
watchband	*biǎodài*	表带
watch out	*xiǎoxīn*	小心
water (n)	*shuǐ*	水
water caltrop	*língjiǎo*	菱角
water chestnut	*bíqì*	荸荠
water lily	*shuǐfúlián*	水浮莲
water polo	*shuǐqiú*	水球
water-skiing	*huáshuǐ yùndòng*	划水运动
watercolors	*shuǐcǎi*	水彩
waterfall	*pùbù*	瀑布
watermelon	*xīguā*	西瓜
wavy	*bōlàngshì*	波浪式
way (direction)	*fāngxiàng*	方向
way (method)	*fāngfǔ*	方法
we	*wǒmen*	我们
weak	*ruò*	弱
wealth	*cáifù*	财富
wealth (symbol)	*lù*	禄
wear	*chuān, dài*	穿，戴
weasel	*huángshǔláng*	黄鼠狼
weather	*tiānqì*	天气
weather forecast	*tiānqì yùbào*	天气预报
weave	*biānzhī*	编织
weaving (n)	*zhīpǐn*	织品
wedding	*hūnlǐ*	婚礼
Wednesday	*xīngqīsān*	星期三
week	*xīngqī*	星期
weekend	*zhōumò*	周末

DICTIONARY

weekly (magazine)	zhōubào	周报
weight-lifting	jǔzhòng	举重
welcome	huānyíng	欢迎
well (adv)	hǎo	好
well (n)	jǐng	井
west	xī	西
West Lake	xīhú	西湖
Western meal	xīcān	西餐
Western menu	xīcān càipǔ	西餐菜谱
Western toilet	zuòshì mǎtǒng	坐式马桶
wet (adj)	shī	湿
what	shénme	什么
wheat	màizi	麦子
wheel	lúnzi	轮子
wheelchair	lúnyǐ	轮椅
when	shénme shíhòu	什么时候
where	nǎli, nǎr	哪里，哪儿
which	nǎge, něige	哪个
whiskey	wēishìjì	威士忌
white	bái	白
White Peony tea	shòuméi chá	寿眉茶
white edible fungus	yín'ěr	银耳
white liquor, Chinese	báijiǔ	白酒
white wine	bái pútáo jiǔ	白葡萄酒
who (question)	shéi	谁
whole	zhěnggè	整个
wholesale	pīfā	批发
why	wèishénme	为什么
wide	kuān	宽
width	kuāndù	宽度
wife	qīzi, fūrén, lǎopó, àirén	妻子，夫人，老婆，爱人
will (determination)	yìzhì	意志
will (future tense)	yào	要
willow tree	liǔshù	柳树
win	yíng	赢
wind (n)	fēng	风
wind instrument (music)	guǎnyuèqì	管乐器
window	chuānghu	窗户
windshield	dǎngfēng bōli	挡风玻璃
windsurfing	fānbǎn yùndòng	帆板运动
windy	yǒufēng	有风

wine	*pútáojiǔ*	葡萄酒
wine glass	*jiǔbēi*	酒杯
winter	*dōngtiān*	冬天
winter melon	*dōngguā*	冬瓜
wintersweet	*làméi*	腊梅
wipe	*cā*	擦
wish (n)	*yuànwàng*	愿望
wishing you...	*zhù nǐ...*	祝你……
within	*zài...yǐnèi*	在……以内
wok	*chǎocài guō*	炒菜锅
woman	*fùnǚ*	妇女
women's bike	*nǚchē*	女车
wonderful	*fēicháng jīngcǎi*	非常精彩
wonton	*húntùn*	馄饨
wood	*mùtou*	木头
woodcut	*mùbǎnhuà*	木板画
wool	*yángmáo*	羊毛
word	*zì*	字
work (art, literature)	*zuòpǐn*	作品
work (job)	*gōngzuò*	工作
work quota	*gōngzuòliàng*	工作量
work unit	*dānwèi*	单位
worker	*gōngrén*	工人
worker's cap	*yāshémào*	鸭舌帽
workshop	*chējiān*	车间
world	*shìjiè*	世界
World War II	*èrcì dàzhàn*	二次大战
worry	*dānxīn*	担心
worse	*gènghuài, gèngzāo*	更坏，更糟
would like to	*xiǎng*	想
wound (n)	*shāngkǒu*	伤口
wrap	*bāo*	包
wrapping paper	*bāozhuāng zhǐ*	包装纸
wrench (hardware)	*bānshou*	扳手
wrestling	*shuāijiāo*	摔跤
wrist	*shǒuwàn*	手腕
write	*xiě*	写
write down	*xiě xià*	写下
writer	*zuòjiā*	作家
writing brush	*máobǐ*	毛笔
writing paper	*xìnzhǐ*	信纸
wrong	*cuò le, bú duì*	错了，不对

DICTIONARY

| X-ray | *X-guāng* | X 光 |
| Xerox (see duplication) | *fùyìn* | 复印 |

yak	*máoniú*	牦牛
Yangtze River	*chángjiāng*	长江
yard (3 feet)	*mǎ*	码
year	*nián*	年
years old (age)	*suì*	岁
yellow	*huáng*	黄
yellow croaker	*huánghuāyú*	黄花鱼
Yellow River	*huánghe*	黄河
Yellow Sea	*huánghǎi*	黄海
yen	*rìyuán*	日元
yesterday	*zuótiān*	昨天
yet	*hái*	还
yogurt	*suānnǎi*	酸奶
you	*nǐ*	你
you (plural)	*nǐmen*	你们
you (polite form)	*nín*	您
young	*niánqīng, xiǎo*	年轻，小
young man	*xiǎo huǒzi*	小伙子
young people	*qīngnián*	青年
young woman	*niánqīng nǚrén*	年轻女人
your	*nǐde*	你的
your (plural)	*nǐmende*	你们的
yurt	*měnggǔbāo*	蒙古包

zebra crosswalk	*bānmǎ xiàn*	斑马线
zero	*líng*	零
zipper	*lāliàn*	拉链
zither, 25-string	*sè*	瑟
zither, 7-string	*gǔqín*	古琴
zither, many-stringed	*zhēng*	筝
zoo	*dòngwùyuán*	动物园

Chinese-English Supplement

This supplement provides English definitions of Chinese terms which are likely to be mentioned to the traveler. In particular, attention has been given to medical vocabulary, names of Chinese foods and products, and words which the traveler might hear in reply to the question *Zhèige shì shén me?* (What is this?)

阿斯匹林	*āsīpǐlín*	aspirin
阿姨	*āyí*	auntie
艾滋病	*àizībìng*	AIDS
鹌鹑	*ānchún*	quail
安眠药	*ānmián yào*	sleeping pill
按摩	*ànmó*	massage
八宝饭	*bābǎofàn*	eight precious rice
拔丝苹果	*básī píngguǒ*	honey crystalized apples
拔牙	*báyá*	extract a tooth
白菜	*báicài*	bok choy; cabbage
白骨精	*báigǔjīng*	WKEs (white collar workers, key member and elite)
白果	*báiguǒ*	ginkgo
白酒	*báijiǔ*	Chinese white liquor
白领	*báilǐng*	white collar workers
白杨树	*báiyángshù*	aspen tree
百	*bǎi*	hundred
百货商店	*bǎihuò shāngdiàn*	department store
柏树	*bǎishù*	cypress tree
斑疹伤寒	*bānzhěn shānghán*	typhus
版画	*bǎnhuà*	print
包车	*bāochē*	hired car
包子	*bāozi*	steamed dumpling
鲍鱼	*bàoyú*	abalone
悲剧	*bēijù*	tragedy
蹦迪	*bèngdi*	Disco
荸荠	*bíqi*	water chestnut
鼻通	*bítōng*	decongestant

鼻子	*bízi*	nose
闭路电视	*bìlù diànshì*	cable TV
避孕用品	*bìyùn yòng pǐn*	contraceptives
便秘	*biànmì*	constipation
宾馆	*bīnguǎn*	guesthouse, hotel
冰球	*bīngqiú*	ice hockey
冰糖葫芦	*bīngtáng húlu*	candied haws
丙纶	*bǐnglún*	acrylic
菠菜	*bōcài*	spinach
博客	*bókè*	blog
播客	*bōkè*	podcast
菠萝	*bōluó*	pineapple
不	*bù*	a negative form, also used as no
不懂	*bùdǒng*	don't understand
不好	*bùhǎo*	not good
不是	*búshì*	not so; not true
不行	*bùxíng*	won't work; no
不锈钢	*búxiùgāng*	stainless steel
补牙	*bǔyá*	fill a tooth
菜豆	*càidòu*	kidney bean
菜花	*càihuā*	cauliflower
彩铃	*cǎilíng*	ring tunes
彩信	*cǎixìn*	graphics
菜心	*càixīn*	cabbage heart
餐厅	*cāntīng*	dining room, restaurant
蚕	*cán*	silkworm
蚕豆	*cándòu*	broad bean
草药	*cǎoyào*	herbal medicine
侧肋	*cèlèi*	side
厕所	*cèsuǒ*	toilet
叉烧包	*chāshāo bāo*	roast pork bun
茶花	*cháhuā*	camellia
产科病房	*chǎnkē bìngfáng*	maternity ward
长寿	*chángshòu*	longevity
肠子	*chángzi*	bowels
拆	*chāi*	pull down; demolish
车间	*chējiān*	workshop
城门	*chéngmén*	city gate
城墙	*chéngqiáng*	city wall
成语	*chéngyǔ*	idiom

充值卡	chōngzhíkǎ	prepaid phone card
抽筋	chōujīn	cramp
出口货	chūkǒu huò	export goods
出血	chūxuè	hemorrhage
传染	chuánrǎn	infection
船闸	chuánzhá	ship lock
春节	chūnjié	Chinese New Year
春卷	chūnjuǎn	spring roll
春运	chūnyùn	passenger transport, during the Spring Festival period
葱	cōng	scallion
葱头	cōngtóu	onion
醋	cù	vinegar
催吐剂	cuītùjì	emetic
村	cūn	village
打的	dǎdi	take a taxi / call a taxi
大白菜	dà báicài	Chinese cabbage
大便	dàbiàn	bowel movement
大道	dàdào	avenue; broad road
大理石	dàlǐshí	marble
大麦	dàmài	barley
大排档	dàpáidàng	small street restaurant
大虾	dàxiā	prawn
大学	dàxué	university
丹顶鹤	dāndǐnghè	red-crowned crane
单位	dānwèi	work unit; organization
单行线	dānxíng xiàn	one-way street
单元	dānyuán	housing unit; doorway
蛋花汤	dànhuātāng	egg-drop soup
刀豆	dāodòu	sword bean
登机牌	dēngjīpái	boarding pass
登记处	dēngjì chù	registration desk
低	dī	low
笛子	dízi	bamboo flute
地铁	dìtiě	subway
地图	dìtú	map
点穴法	diǎnxuèfǎ	acupressure
电报	diànbào	telegram
电报挂号	diànbào guàhào	cable address
电传	diànchuán	telex

SUPPLEMENT

电传挂号	*diànchuán guàhào*	telex call number
电疗	*diànliáo*	electrotherapy
电子地图	*diànzǐ dìtú*	electronic map, e-map
电子邮件	*diànzǐ yóujiàn*	email
貂	*diāo*	marten
丁香	*dīngxiāng*	lilac
丁香酒	*dīngxiāng jiǔ*	clove wine
丁字路口	*dīngzi lùkou*	T-intersection
定额	*dìng'é*	quota
冬菇	*dōnggū*	black mushroom
冬瓜	*dōngguā*	winter melon
豆瓣酱	*dòubàn jiàng*	hot bean sauce
豆腐	*dòufu*	beancurd, tofu
豆腐干	*dòufu gān*	dried beancurd
豆浆	*dòujiāng*	soybean milk
豆沙	*dòushā*	sweetened bean paste
豆芽	*dòuyá*	bean sprout
豆子	*dòuzi*	bean
堵车	*dǔchē*	traffic jam
杜鹃花	*dùjuānhuā*	azalea
短信	*duǎnxìn*	text message
对	*duì*	correct
对不起	*duìbuqǐ*	excuse me, sorry
恶心	*ěxīn*	nauseous
儿科	*érkē*	pediatrics department
耳鼻喉科	*ěrbíhóu kē*	ear-nose-throat department
二胡	*èrhú*	2-string fiddle
发抖	*fādǒu*	shiver
发炎	*fāyán*	inflammation, infection
蕃茄	*fānqié*	tomato
饭	*fàn*	rice
饭店	*fàndiàn*	hotel; restaurant
饭馆	*fànguǎn*	restaurant
饭后	*fànhòu*	after meals
饭前	*fànqián*	before meals
房间	*fángjiān*	room
防疫证	*fángyì zhèng*	vaccination certificate
放射科	*fàngshèkē*	radiology department
翡翠	*fěicuì*	jadeite

肺	fèi	lung
肺结核	fèi jiéhé	tuberculosis
肺炎	fèiyán	pneumonia
坟墓	fénmù	tomb
风湿病	fēngshī bìng	rheumatism
凤仙花	fèngxiānhuā	touch-me-not
佛经	fójīng	sutra
福	fú	symbol for luck
服务费	fúwùfèi	service fee
服务台	fúwùtái	service desk; reception
服务员	fúwùyuán	service attendant
服装店	fúzhuāng diàn	clothing store
妇科	fùkē	gynecology department
副食品	fùshí pǐn	nonstaple food
腹泻	fùxiè	diarrhea
复制品	fùzhìpǐn	reproduction
芥菜	gàicài	leaf mustard
芥蓝	gàilán	Chinese broccoli
肝	gān	liver
干咸鱼	gān xián yú	dried minced fish
干杯!	gānbēi	Bottoms up! Cheers!
干贝	gānbèi	scallop
肝炎	gānyán	hepatitis
柑子	gānzi	mandarin orange
橄榄	gǎnlǎn	olive
感冒	gǎnmào	cold; flu
高	gāo	high
高尔夫	gāo'ěrfū	golf
高粱	gāoliáng	sorghum
膏药	gāoyào	medicated plaster
高原	gāoyuán	highland
鸽子	gēzi	pigeon
隔离病房	gélí bìngfáng	isolation ward
蛤蜊	gélí	clams
公安局	gōng'ānjú	Public Security Bureau
功夫	gōngfu	a martial art; gung-fu
公斤	gōngjīn	kilogram
公里	gōnglǐ	kilometer
公路	gōnglù	highway
公顷	gōngqǐng	hectare
公务员	gōngwùyuán	civil servant

SUPPLEMENT

工艺美术	gōngyì měishù	arts and crafts
公寓	gōngyù	apartment
工资	gōngzī	salary
工作量	gōngzuò liàng	work quota
够了	gòule	enough
鼓楼	gǔlóu	drum tower
古琴	gǔqín	7-string zither
骨头	gǔtou	bone
挂面	guàmiàn	vermicelli
观察室	guānchá shì	observation ward
关节	guānjié	joints
关节炎	guānjié yán	arthritis
关系	guānxi	connection, relation
规定	guīdìng	regulation
桂花	guìhuā	cassia
桂花酒	guìhuā jiǔ	cassia wine
锅贴	guōtiē	fried dumplings
国画	guóhuà	traditional Chinese painting
国务院	guówùyuàn	state council
过来	guòlái	come over; come here; come up
过敏症	guòmǐn zhèng	allergy
哈密瓜	hāmìguā	Hami melon
海关申报单	hǎiguān shēnbào dān	customs declaration
海狸	hǎilí	beaver
海米	hǎimǐ	dried shrimps
海参	hǎishēn	sea cucumber
海棠	hǎitáng	Chinese crabapple
海鲜	hǎixiān	seafood
海蜇	hàizhé	jellyfish
含片	hánpiàn	throat lozenges
汉，汉族	hàn. hànzú	the dominant Chinese ethnic group; Han
汗	hàn	sweat
汉语	hànyǔ	Chinese language
蚝	háo	oyster
蚝油	háoyóu	oyster sauce
好不好	hǎobùhǎo	Is it good or bad? How is it?
好莱坞	hǎoláiwū	Hollywood

鹤	hè	crane
荷花	héhuā	lotus
核桃	hétao	walnut
和弦铃声	héxuán língshēng	polyphonic ring tunes
红茶	hóngchá	black tea
红绿灯	hónglǜdēng	traffic light
红烧	hóngshāo	braised in brown sauce
红薯	hóngshǔ	sweet potato
喉咙	hóulóng	throat
后门	hòumén	back door; the unofficial way
忽必烈	hūbìliè	Kublai Khan
胡同	hútóng	alley; lane. Usually refers to old residential streets in Beijing
沪剧	hùjù	Shanghai Opera
护照	hùzhào	passport
花菜	huācài	cauliflower
花粉热	huāfěn rè	hay fever
花卷	huājuǎn	steamed twisted roll
花生	huāshēng	peanut
华侨	huáqiáo	overseas Chinese
化疗	huàliáo	chemotherapy
化纤	huàxiān	synthetic
槐树	huáishù	locust tree
怀孕	huáiyùn	pregnant
磺胺	huáng'ān	sulfa
黄豆	huángdòu	soybean
黄瓜	huángguā	cucumber
黄花鱼	huánghuāyú	yellow croaker
黄金周	huángjīnzhōu	golden weeks, week-long national holidays
黄鼠狼	huángshǔláng	weasel
昏迷	hūnmí	coma
馄饨	húntùn	wonton
火车	huǒchē	train
火车时刻表	huǒchē shíkèbiǎo	train schedule or timetable
火锅	huǒguō	hot pot
火腿	huǒtuǐ	ham
霍乱	huòluàn	cholera

SUPPLEMENT

机场费	jīchǎng fèi	airport departure tax
鸡冠花	jīguānhuā	cock's comb
肌肉	jīròu	muscle
急救站	jíjiù zhàn	first-aid station
集市	jíshì	village fair
集邮	jíyóu	stamp collecting
急诊室	jízhěn shì	emergency room
脊椎	jǐzhuī	spine
家乡	jiāxiāng	native place
夹竹桃	jiāzhútáo	oleander
驾驶执照	jiàshǐ zhízhào	driver's license
煎饼	jiānbǐng	crepe, egg pancake
减价	jiǎnjià	price reduction
简谱	jiǎnpǔ	numbered music notation
检疫	jiǎnyì	quarantine
健康表	jiànkāng biǎo	health declaration
健美操	jiànměi cāo	aerobics
江	jiāng	river (also a surname, i.e. Jiang Zemin)
豇豆	jiāngdòu	green long bean
奖金	jiǎngjīn	bonus
酱油	jiàngyóu	soy sauce
饺子	jiǎozi	boiled dumplings, ravioli
节目	jiémù	program; event
结账	jiézhàng	settle the bill
借光	jièguāng	excuse me, make way
芥末	jièmo	mustard
斤	jīn	traditional unit of weight, now 0.5 kg
筋	jīn	tendon
金桔	jīnjú	kumquat
金丝猴	jīnsīhóu	golden-haired monkey
金鱼	jīnyú	goldfish
金针	jīnzhēn	day-lily bud
进口货	jìnkǒu huò	import goods
京胡	jīnghú	Beijing Opera fiddle
经济日报	jīngjì rìbào	*Economic Daily*
京剧	jīngjù	Beijing Opera
痉挛	jīngluán	convulsion
精神病	jīngshénbìng	psychosis
精神分裂	jīngshén fēnliè	schizophrenia

静脉注射	jìngmài zhùshè	intravenous injection
酒	jiǔ	alcoholic beverage
韭菜	jiǔcài	Chinese chives
酒精	jiǔjīng	alcohol
居留证	jūliú zhèng	residence permit
局部麻醉	júbù mázuì	local anesthesia
菊花	júhuā	chrysanthemum
剧场	jùchǎng	theater
卡拉OK包间	karaoke bāojiān	karaoke room
开水	kāishuǐ	boiled water
凯乐	kǎiyuè	Hyatt
抗生素	kàngshēngsù	antibiotic
烤乳猪	kǎorǔzhū	roast suckling pig
咳嗽	késou	cough
可怜	kělián	pity; have pity; pitiful
空调	kōngtiáo	air-conditioning; air-conditioned
口水	kǒushuǐ	saliva
苦瓜	kǔguā	bitter gourd
块	kuài	basic unit of money: yuan
快点	kuài diǎn	a little faster; hurry up
宽带	kuāndài	broadband
奎宁	kuíníng	quinine
溃疡	kuìyáng	ulcer
昆曲	kūnqǔ	Kunshan Opera
拉肚子	lā dùzi	diarrhea
辣酱	làjiàng	hot sauce
辣椒	làjiāo	chilli pepper
腊梅	làméi	wintersweet
腊肉	làròu	cured meat
兰花	lánhuā	orchid
篮球	lánqiú	basketball
劳驾	láojia	excuse me, make way
老家	lǎojiā	ancestral place
老外	lǎowài	foreigner
肋骨	lèigǔ	rib
梨	lí	pear
里	lǐ	traditional unit of distance, now 0.5 km
理发店	lǐfà diàn	barbershop

SUPPLEMENT

李子	*lǐzi*	plum
痢疾	*lìji*	dysentery
荔枝	*lìzhī*	lychee
栗子	*lìzi*	chestnut
莲花	*liánhuā*	lotus
莲藕	*lián'ǒu*	lotus root
莲子	*liánzǐ*	lotus seed
烈士	*lièshì*	martyr
菱角	*língjiǎo*	water caltrop
零钱	*língqián*	coins, small bills
零售	*língshòu*	retail
流感	*liúgǎn*	flu
柳树	*liǔshù*	willow tree
龙井茶	*lóngjǐng chá*	Dragon Well tea
龙虾	*lóngxiā*	lobster
龙眼	*lóngyǎn*	longan fruit
路	*lù*	road; path
禄	*lù*	symbol for wealth
鹿	*lù*	deer
路口	*lùkǒu*	intersection, crossroad
鹿茸	*lùróng*	pilose antler
旅馆	*lǚguǎn*	hostel
旅社	*lǚshè*	hostel
旅行社	*lǚxíngshè*	travel service
绿茶	*lùchá*	green tea
绿豆	*lùdòu*	mung bean
萝卜	*luóbo*	turnip
麻花	*máhuā*	fried dough twists
麻将	*májiàng*	mah-jong
麻油	*máyóu*	sesame oil
麻疹	*mázhěn*	measles
麻醉	*mázuì*	anesthesia
吗啡	*mǎfēi*	morphine
马克·波罗	*mǎkè bōluó*	Marco Polo
玛瑙	*mǎnǎo*	agate
马马虎虎	*mǎmǎhūhū*	so-so
买单	*mǎidan*	pay the bill (in a restaurant)
脉搏	*màibó*	pulse
麦当劳	*màidāngláo*	McDonald's
麦子	*màizi*	wheat

馒头	mántou	steamed bread
慢车	mànchē	local bus or train
慢性	mànxìng	chronic
芒果	mángguǒ	mango
毛	máo	dime, a tenth of a yuan. Also jiǎo 角
牦牛	máoniú	yak
茅台	máotái	Maotai liquor
没办法, 没办法啦	méibànfǎ, méibànfǎla	no way; no means; nothing to be done about it
玫瑰花	méiguìhuā	rose
梅花	méihuā	plum blossom
没有, 没有啦	méiyǒu, méiyǒula	don't have, a universal no
没有问题	méiyǒuwèntí	no problem
米	mǐ	meter
米粉	mǐfěn	rice-flour noodles
米老鼠	mǐlǎoshǔ	Mickey Mouse
棉	mián	cotton
免费	miǎnfèi	free of charge
面条	miàntiáo	noodles
蘑菇	mógu	mushroom
摩托	mótuō	motor; motorcycle
墨	mò	ink stick
末班车	mò bān chē	last bus or train
墨斗鱼	mòdǒuyú	cuttlefish
茉莉花茶	mòlì huāchá	jasmine tea
牡丹	mǔdān	peony
拇指族	mǔzhǐzú	thumb people (SMS text lovers)
墓地	mùdì	burial grounds
奶茶	nǎichá	milk tea, popular in Mongolian and Tibetan regions
男厕	náncè	men's room
男同性恋, 同志	nántóngxìngliàn, tóngzhì	gay
脑膜炎	nǎomó yán	meningitis
脑炎	nǎoyán	encephalitis
内部	nèibù	inside; internal; restricted or classified

SUPPLEMENT

年糕	niángāo	glutinous rice cake
年画	niánhuà	New Year painting
牛肉	niúròu	beef
暖冬	nuǎndōng	warm winter
女厕	nǚcè	women's room
女同性恋	nǚtóngxìngliàn	lesbian
女同志	nǚtóngzhì	lesbian
疟疾	nüèji	malaria
藕	ǒu	lotus root
呕吐	ǒutù	vomit
排骨	páigǔ	sparerib
牌楼	páilóu	memorial arch
排球	páiqiú	volleyball
派出所	pàichūsuǒ	police station
盘尼西林	pánníxīlín	penicillin
螃蟹	pángxiè	crab
泡菜	pàocài	pickled vegetables
盆地	péndì	land basin
盆景	pénjǐng	bonsai
朋友	péngyǒu	friend
批发	pīfā	wholesale
霹雳舞	pīlìwǔ	breakdancing
皮蛋	pídàn	thousand-year egg, preserved duck egg
皮肤科	pífūkē	dermatology department
琵琶	pípá	4-string lute
枇杷	pípá	loquat
皮下	píxià	hypodermic
皮鞋	píxié	leather shoes
皮影	píyǐng	shadow puppet
皮疹	pízhěn	rash
片	piàn	tablet; pill; piece
票	piào	ticket
贫血症	pínxuě zhèng	anemia
拼音	pīnyīn	official Romanization of Putonghua, giving phonetic spelling
评剧	píngjù	Pingju Opera
平原	píngyuán	plains
瓶子	píngzi	jar; bottle; traveling tea cup

破伤风	pò shāngfēng	tetanus
葡萄	pútáo	grape
葡萄干	pútáo gān	raisin
葡萄糖	pútáo táng	glucose
普洱茶	pǔ ěr chá	Puer tea
普通舱	pǔtōngcāng	economy class
普通话	pǔtōnghuà	modern standard Chinese language; common speech; Mandarin
瀑布	pùbù	waterfall
祁门红茶	qímén hóngchá	Keemun tea
气喘	qìchuǎn	asthma
气功	qìgōng	breath energy exercise
千	qiān	thousand
千克	qiānkè	kilogram
签证	qiānzhèng	visa
蔷薇	qiángwēi	hedge rose
桥	qiáo	bridge
茄子	qiézi	eggplant
芹菜	qíncài	celery
青光眼	qīngguāng yǎn	laucoma
青椒	qīngjiāo	green pepper
青稞	qīngkē	barley
青霉素	qīngméisù	penicillin
青蛙	qīngwā	frog
清真	qīngzhēn	Moslem
晴纶	qínglún	polyester
秋海棠	qiūhǎitáng	begonia
全国	quánguó	whole country; all China
全身麻醉	quánshēn mázuì	general anesthesia
人民币	rénmínbì	the Chinese currency, RMB
人民日报	rénmín rìbào	*People's Daily*
人参	rénshēn	ginseng
人造丝	rénzào sī	rayon
日报	rìbào	daily newspaper
榕树	róngshù	banyan tree
肉松	ròusōng	shredded dried meat
阮	ruǎn	Chinese banjo

SUPPLEMENT

软膏	ruǎngāo	ointment
软件工程师	ruǎnjiàn gōngchéngshī	software engineer
软卧	ruǎnwò	soft-sleeper
软席	ruǎnxí	soft-seat
三环	sānhuán	Third Ring Road
三轮车	sānlúnchē	pedicab (pedal-powered tricycle taxi); tricycle truck
三弦琴	sānxián qín	3-string guitar
桑树	sāngshù	mulberry tree
嗓子	sǎngzi	throat; voice
瑟	sè	25-string zither
山羊	shānyáng	goat
山楂	shānzhā	haw
鳝鱼	shànyú	eel
上	shàng	upper; on top
商店	shāngdiàn	shop
伤寒	shānghán	typhoid
伤口	shāngkǒu	wound (n)
上网	shàngwǎng	online; using Internet
烧饼	shāobǐng	sesame biscuit
蛇	shé	snake
猞猁	shèlì	lynx
神经病学	shénjīngbìng xué	neurology
神经症	shénjīngzhèng	neurosis
肾	shèn	kidney
升	shēng	liter
笙	shēng	Chinese mouth organ
生姜	shēngjiāng	ginger
省	shěng	province
师傅	shīfu	master worker
失眠	shīmián	insomnia
石版画	shíbǎnhuā	lithograph
实际	shíjì	practical, realistic
石榴	shíliu	pomegranate
食品店	shípǐn diàn	grocery store
食物中毒	shíwù zhòngdú	food poisoning
柿子	shìzi	persimmon
收款处	shōukuǎnchù	cashier's booth
首班车	shǒu bān chē	first bus or train
手风琴	shǒufēngqín	accordion

手机	*shǒujī*	mobile or cell phone
手术室	*shǒushù shì*	operation room
寿	*shòu*	symbol for longevity
寿眉茶	*shòuméi chá*	White Peony tea
售票处	*shòupiào chù*	ticket office
书店	*shūdiàn*	bookstore
书记处	*shūjìchù*	secretariat
叔叔	*shūshu*	uncle
数码相机	*shùmǎ xiàngjī*	digital camera
涮羊肉	*shuànyángròu*	Mongolian hot pot
水貂	*shuǐdiāo*	mink
睡莲	*shuìlián*	water lily
水饺	*shuǐjiǎo*	ravioli, boiled dumplings
水獭	*shuǐtǎ*	otter
水仙	*shuǐxiān*	narcissus
税	*shuì*	tax
睡前	*shuìqián*	before sleep
四合院	*sìhéyuàn*	traditional Chinese courtyard
四环	*sìhuán*	Fourth Ring Road
四季豆	*sìjìdòu*	string bean
松	*sōng*	pine tree
松花蛋	*sōnghuādàn*	thousand-year egg
宿舍	*sùshè*	dormitory; housing
酸	*suān*	sore; sour
酸辣汤	*suānlà tāng*	hot-and-sour soup
酸奶	*suānnǎi*	yogurt
蒜	*suàn*	garlic
算盘	*suànpán*	Chinese abacus
孙中山	*sūn zhōngshān*	Sun Yat-sen
唢呐	*suǒnà*	Chinese cornet
台风	*táifēng*	typhoon
太贵，太贵了	*tàiguì. tàiguìle*	too expensive
太监	*tàijiān*	eunuch
滩羊	*tānyáng*	argali sheep
汤	*tāng*	soup
汤面	*tāngmiàn*	soup noodles
唐老鸭	*tánglǎoyā*	Donald Duck
糖尿病	*tángniàobìng*	diabetes
桃子	*táozi*	peach
特快	*tèkuài*	express

SUPPLEMENT

疼	*téng*	pain
体温	*tǐwēn*	temperature
体育馆	*tǐyùguǎn*	gymnasium
天知道	*tiānzhīdào*	heaven knows
甜菜	*tiáncài*	beet
铁观音茶	*tiěguānyīn chá*	Iron Goddess of Mercy tea
铁路	*tiělù*	railroad
同性恋，同志	*tóngxìngliàn, tóngzhì*	homosexual
同志	*tóngzhì*	comrade
痛苦	*tòngkǔ*	pain
头班车	*tóu bān chē*	first bus or train
头等舱	*tóuděngcāng*	first class
头晕	*tóuyūn*	dizzy
兔子	*tùzi*	rabbit
推拿	*tuīná*	massage
退热	*tuìrè*	antipyretic
吞咽	*tūnyàn*	swallow
外宾	*wàibīn*	foreign guest
外地人	*wàidìrén*	outside person, not a local
外汇	*wàihuì*	foreign exchange
外国人	*wàiguórén*	foreigner
外科	*wàikē*	surgery department
外用	*wàiyòng*	external use
湾	*wān*	gulf or bay
晚安	*wǎnān*	good night
豌豆黄	*wāndòu huáng*	pea-flour cake
万	*wàn*	ten thousand
网吧	*wǎngbā*	Internet cafe
网恋	*wǎngliàn*	Cyber-love affair
网上聊天	*wǎngshàng liáotiān*	chatting on the Internet; Cyber chatting
网友	*wǎngyǒu*	Netizens
危急	*wēijí*	critical
围棋	*wéiqí*	go
喂	*wèi*	Hey; hello (answering telephone)
胃穿孔	*wèi chuānkǒng*	gastric perforation
胃疼	*wèiténg*	stomachache
胃炎	*wèiyán*	gastritis

蚊子	wénzi	mosquito
问讯处	wènxún chù	information desk
莴笋	wōsǔn	asparagus lettuce
乌龟	wūguī	tortoise
乌龙茶	wūlóng chá	oolong tea
乌贼	wūzéi	cuttlefish
无	wú	nothing; nil; not have
无轨电车	wúguǐ diànchē	trolley
无花果	wúhuāguǒ	fig
梧桐树	wútóngshù	Chinese parasol tree
武警	wǔjǐng	armed police
五粮液	wǔliángyè	five-grain liquor
武术	wǔshù	martial arts
舞厅	wǔtīng	dance hall
五线谱	wǔxiàn pǔ	5-line musical staff
希尔顿	xī ěrdùn	Hilton
西餐	xīcān	Western meal
稀饭	xīfàn	rice porridge, congee
西红柿	xīhóngshì	tomato
西药	xīyào	Western medicine
喜	xǐ	symbol for happiness
囍	xǐ	double happiness
喜来登	xǐláidēng	Sheraton
喜玛拉雅山	xǐmǎlāyǎ shān	Himalayas
虾	xiā	shrimp
下	xià	lower; below; down
咸鸭蛋	xián yādàn	salted duck egg
衔接航班	xiánjiē hángbān	connecting flight
县	xiàn	county
乡	xiāng	township
香菜	xiāngcài	coriander
香格里拉	xiānggélǐlā	Shangri-La
香菇	xiānggū	black mushroom
香酥鸡	xiāngsū jī	fried crisp chicken
香酥鸭	xiāngsū yā	crispy duck
香油	xiāngyóu	sesame oil
香肠	xiāngcháng	sausage
象棋	xiàngqí	Chinese chess
相声	xiàngsheng	cross talk
箫	xiāo	vertical bamboo flute
消毒膏	xiāodú gāo	antiseptic cream

SUPPLEMENT

消化	xiāohuà	digestion
小灵通	xiǎolíngtōng	Little Smart , a cell phone service provided by a local telecom company with limited coverage; Also called PAS
小笼包	xiǎolóng bāo	small steamed dumpling
小米	xiǎomǐ	millet
小山羊皮	xiǎoshānyáng pí	kidskin
小偷	xiǎotōu	thief (sneak thief, not a robber)
小熊猫	xiǎoxióngmāo	lesser panda
小羊皮	xiǎoyáng pí	lambskin
泻药	xièyào	cathartic
新石器时代	xīn shíqì shídài	Neolithic era
新华书店	xīnhuá shūdiàn	the government bookstore; New China
心悸	xīnjì	palpitation
心绞痛	xīnjiǎotòng	angina pectoris
心理学	xīnlǐxué	psychology
心力衰竭	xīnlì shuāijié	cardiac failure
心脏病发作	xīnzàngbìng fāzuò	heart attack
腥红热	xīnghóngrè	scarlet fever
杏	xìng	apricot
幸福	xìngfú	happiness
杏仁	xìngrén	almond
杏仁茶	xìngrénchá	almond-flour tea
杏仁豆腐	xìngrén dòufu	almond gelatin
性骚扰	xìngsāorǎo	sexual harassment
休克	xiūkè	shock
绣球花	xiùqiú huā	geranium
岫玉	xiùyù	Manchurian jasper
宣纸	xuānzhǐ	Xuan paper
血	xuè	blood
血压	xuèyā	blood pressure
血型	xuèxíng	blood type
熏鱼	xūnyú	smoked fish
牙科医生	yákē yīshēng	dentist
亚麻布	yàmá bù	linen
腌黄瓜	yān huánggua	pickled cucumber
阉鸡	yānjī	capon

研究所	yánjiūsuǒ	research institute
岩溶	yánróng	karst
眼科	yǎnkē	ophthalmology department
眼药水	yǎnyàoshuǐ	eye drops
咽	yàn	swallow
砚台	yàntái	ink slab
羊毛	yángmáo	wool
杨梅	yángméi	red bayberry
扬琴	yángqín	dulcimer
羊肉	yángròu	mutton
痒	yǎng	itch
氧气	yǎngqì	oxygen
样品	yàngpǐn	sample
腰鼓	yāogǔ	waist drum
腰果	yāoguǒ	cashew nut
腰疼	yāoténg	lumbago
药	yào	medicine
药方	yàofāng	prescription
药房	yàofáng	pharmacy
药丸	yàowán	pill
椰子	yēzi	coconut
夜班车	yèbān chē	night bus
腋下	yèxià	underarm
亿	yì	hundred million
一点点	yìdiǎndiǎn	a little; a few
一个人	yígè rén	one person; alone; by yourself
医生	yīshēng	doctor
医院	yīyuàn	hospital
译制片	yìzhì piàn	dubbed film
音乐厅	yīnyuè tīng	concert hall
银耳	yín'ěr	white edible fungus
银杏	yínxìng	ginkgo
饮料	yǐnliào	beverage
印泥	yìnní	red paste for seals
英里	yīnglǐ	mile
樱桃	yīngtáo	cherry
英文	yīngwén	English language
硬卧	yìngwò	hard-sleeper
硬坐	yìngzuò	hard-seat
油菜	yóucài	rape

SUPPLEMENT

邮局	yóujú	post office
邮票	yóupiào	postage stamp
油条	yóutiáo	fried cruller
鱿鱼	yóuyú	squid
柚子	yòuzi	pomelo
鱼	yú	fish
鱼翅汤	yúchì tāng	shark's fin soup
榆树	yúshù	elm tree
羽毛球	yǔmáoqiú	badminton
豫剧	yùjù	Henan Opera
芋头	yùtou	taro
元	yuán	the unit of RMB, Chinese currency
鸳鸯	yuānyang	mandarin ducks
原作	yuánzuò	original
月光族	yuèguāngzú	earn-it-spend-it people
月季	yuèjì	Chinese rose
月经	yuèjīng	menstruation
越剧	yuèjù	Shaoxing Opera
粤剧	yuèjù	Cantonese Opera
月票	yuèpiào	monthly ticket
月琴	yuèqín	4-string mandolin
芸豆	yúndòu	kidney bean
枣	zǎo	date
澡堂	zǎotáng	bathhouse
榨菜	zhàcài	hot pickled mustard tuber
宅急送	zháijísòng	courier service
站台票	zhàntáipiào	platform ticket (at the train station)
站票	zhànpiào	standing ticket (no seat or berth)
占线	zhànxiàn	busy line
樟树	zhāngshù	camphor tree
招待所	zhāodàisuǒ	guesthouse
针灸	zhēnjiǔ	acupuncture
真丝	zhēnsī	silk
珍珠	zhēnzhū	pearl
诊断	zhěnduàn	diagnosis
镇	zhèn	town
镇静剂	zhènjìngjì	tranquilizer
筝	zhēng	many-stringed zither

政治局	zhèngzhìjú	political bureau
症状	zhèngzhuàng	symptom
支气管炎	zhīqìguǎn yán	bronchitis
止疼药	zhǐténg yào	pain-killer
中	zhōng	center; middle
中餐	zhōngcān	Chinese meal
中国	zhōngguó	the country of China (short name)
钟楼	zhōnglóu	bell tower
中铺	zhōngpù	middle berth (on ticket)
中文	zhōngwén	the Chinese language
中药	zhōngyào	traditional Chinese medicine, TCM
肿胀	zhǒngzhàng	swelling
中暑	zhòngshǔ	sunstroke
粥	zhōu	porridge, congee
州	zhōu	state; prefecture
珠穆朗玛峰	zhūmùlángmǎfēng	Mount Qomolangma
猪肉	zhūròu	pork
竹笋	zhúsǔn	bamboo shoot
注射	zhùshè	injection
住院处	zhùyuàn chù	inpatient department
紫貂	zǐdiāo	sable
走	zǒu	go (away)
足底按摩	zúdǐ ànmo	foot massage
足球	zúqiú	soccer
钻石	zuànshí	diamond

Appendix A

Numbers and Quantities

Cardinal Numbers

Number			Comments
0	零	líng	*1 is read as yāo when
1	一	yī*	stating a phone number,
2	二	èr**	room number, bus num-
3	三	sān	ber, and such identifica-
4	四	sì	tions.
5	五	wǔ	**2 is usually read as
6	六	liù	liǎng when referring to
7	七	qī	quantity. For example,
8	八	bā	"two people" would be
9	九	jiǔ	liǎng gè rén.
10	十	shí	
20	二十	èrshí	two tens
30	三十	sānshí	three tens
40...	四十	sìshí	four tens...
11	十一	shíyī	ten and one
12	十二	shí èr	ten and two
13...	十三	shísān	ten and three...
21	二十一	èrshíyī	twenty and one
22	二十二	èrshíèr	twenty and two
23...	二十三	èrshísān	twenty and three...
100	百	bǎi	
1,000	千	qiān	
10,000	万	wàn	
1,000,000	百万	bǎiwàn	

Ordinal Numbers

Ordinal number is formed by inserting *dì* in front of the number.

first	*dì yī*	第一
second	*dì èr*	第二
third...	*dì sān*	第三
first one	*dì yīgè*	第一个
first time	*dì yīcì*	第一次

Fractions

Except for one-half, *yí bàn*, fractions are formed in the pattern (D) *fēnzhī* (N) with D being the denominator and N the numerator.

Examples:

1/3	*sān fēnzhī yī*	三分之一
1/4	*sì fēnzhī yī*	四分之一
3/4	*sì fēnzhī sān*	四分之三
2/5	*wǔ fēnzhī èr*	五分之二

Percentages

To form a percentage, use the pattern *bǎi fēn zhī* (P) with P being the percentage.

Examples:

25%	*bǎi fēnzhī èrshí wǔ*	百分之二十五
80%	*bǎi fēnzhī bāshí*	百分之八十
100%	*bǎi fēnzhī yìbǎi*	百分之一百

Appendix B

Measure Words

Measure Word		What It Modifies	Examples
bǎ	把	knives, chairs, keys	sān bǎ dāo (3 knives) yì bǎ yǐzi (a chair)
běn	本	books	yì běn xiǎoshuō (a novel) liǎng běn zìdiǎn (2 dictionaries)
duì	对	pairs, couples	yí duì huāpíng (a pair of vases) sān duì fūfù (3 married couples)
fèn	份	portions, printed matter, newspapers	yí fèn zhōngguó rìbào (a copy of *China Daily*)
fēng	封	letters (mail)	liǎng fēng xìn (2 letters)
gè	个	most things	sān gè rén (3 people) yí gè píngguǒ (an apple) wǔ gè xīngqī (5 weeks)
jiān	间	rooms	liǎng jiān wòshì (2 bedrooms)
jiàn	件	clothing, suitcases	yí jiàn chènshān (a shirt) liǎng jiàn xíngli (2 suitcases)
kē	棵	trees	yì kē sōng shù (a pine tree)
kuài	块	rectangular objects, money	yí kuài féizào (a bar of soap) sì kuài miànbāo

			(4 slices of bread)
			shí kuài qián (10 yuan)
liàng	辆	vehicles	*yí liàng zìxíngchē* (a bicycle)
			liǎng liàng qìchē (2 cars)
pán	盘	flat, circular objects	*zhèi pán cídài* (this tape cassette)
			wǔ pán cài (5 dishes of food)
shuāng	双	pairs related to hands and feet	*yì shuāng píxié* (a pair of leather shoes)
			sì shuāng shǒutào (4 pairs of gloves)
tái	台	machines	*yì tái dǎzìjī* (a typewriter)
			yì tái jìsuánjī (a computer)
tiáo	条	long, linear objects	*yì tiáo kùzi* (a pair of pants)
			yì tiáo jiē (a street)
			sān tiáo yú (3 fish)
zhāng	张	sheets, such as paper, tickets, photos, maps	*liǎng zhāng piào* (2 tickets)
			jǐ zhāng zhǐ (some sheets of paper)
zhī	只	animals	*sān zhī niǎo* (3 birds)
			yì zhī lǎohǔ (a tiger)
zhī	支	writing tools	*yì zhī máobǐ* (a Chinese brush)
			sān zhī gāngbǐ (3 fountain pens)

Appendix C

Expressions of Time

Divisions of the Day

morning	*zǎoshang, zǎochén*	早上，早晨
mid-morning	*shàngwǔ*	上午
noon	*zhōngwǔ*	中午
afternoon	*xiàwǔ*	下午
evening	*wǎnshang*	晚上
night	*yèlǐ*	夜里

Hours and Minutes

hour	*xiǎoshí, zhōngtóu*	小时，钟头
half	*bàn*	半
quarter	*kè*	刻
o'clock	*diǎn, diǎnzhōng*	点，点钟
minute	*fēn, fēnzhōng*	分，分钟
less	*chà*	差

Examples:

3 hours	*sān gè xiǎoshí*
3 1/2 hours	*sān gè bàn xiǎoshí*
8:00	*bā diǎn, bā diǎn zhōng*
8:05	*bā diǎn líng wǔ*
8:10	*bā diǎn shí fēn*
8:15	*bā diǎn yí kè*
8:30	*bā diǎn bàn*
8:50	*bā diǎn wǔshí, jiu diǎn chà shí fēn*
9:00 am	*zǎoshang jiǔ diǎn*
9:00 pm	*wǎnshang jiǔ diǎn*
2:00 pm	*xiàwǔ liǎng diǎn*
2:00 am	*yèlǐ liǎng diǎn*

Appendix D

Conversion Charts

Measures

The metric system is widely used in China, along with a few traditional Chinese units of measure. The chart below gives rough equivalences among the various systems. The Chinese translations of the metric and American units, such as shēng for liter, can be found in the dictionary.

Chinese Unit	Metric Unit	American Unit

Length

Chinese Unit	Metric Unit	American Unit
	1cm	0.4 in
	2.5 cm	1in
	30.5 cm	1ft
1 chǐ 尺	33.3 cm	13.1in
	91.4 cm	1yd
3 chǐ	1m	39.4 in
1 lǐ 里	0.5 km	0.3 mi
2 lǐ	1 km	0.6 mi
	1.6 km	1m

Area

Chinese Unit	Metric Unit	American Unit
	6.5 sq cm	1 sq in
	929 sq cm	1 sq ft
	0.8 sq m	1 sq yd
	1 sq m	1,550 sq in
1 mǔ 亩	674.5 sq m	807 sq yd
6 mǔ	4,047 sq m	1 acre
15 mǔ	1 ha	2.5 acres
	1 sq km	0.4 sq mi
	2.6 sq km	1 sq mi

Weight

1qián 钱	5 g	0.2 oz
	28.4 g	1oz
1liǎng 两	50 g	1.8 oz
	454 g	1 lb
1jīn 斤	500 g	1.1 lb
2jīn	1kg	2.2 lb
	0.9MT	1 ton
2,000jīn	1MT	2,204.6 lb

Capacity

1cl	0.3 fl oz	1.1 l	1 qt (dry)
47.3 cl	1 pt (fl)	3.8 l	1 gal (fl)
55 cl	1 pt (dry)	8.8 l	1 pk
94.6 cl	1 qt (fl)	35.2 l	1 bu
1 l	1.1 qt (fl)	1 hl	2.8 bu
1 l	0.9 qt (dry)		

Temperature

To calculate the Fahrenheit equivalent of a centigrade temperature, use this formula:

$°F = 32 + 1.8 × °C$

°C	°F
35	95
30	86
25	77
20	68
15	59
10	50
5	41
0	32
-5	23
-10	14
-15	5
-20	-4

Appendix E

Money

Chinese Currency

The Chinese currency is called *rénmínbì* (RMB), with the basic unit being the *yuán* (¥). One-tenth of a yuan is called a *jiǎo*. One-hundredth of a yuan is called a *fēn*.

In spoken Chinese, a yuan is often called a *kuài* and a *jiǎo* is called a *máo*. When stating a price, the last identifying word "mao" or "fen" is left out.

Examples:

¥15.00	*shíwǔ kuài*
¥15.65	*shíwǔ kuài liù máo wǔ* (no "fen")
¥ 1.50	*yí kuài wǔ* (no "mao")
¥ 0.30	*sān máo*
¥ 0.32	*sān máo èr* (no "fen")
¥ 0.02	*liǎng fēn*

Foreign Currencies

US dollar	*měiyuán*	美元
Canadian dollar	*jiāyuán*	加元
Australian dollar	*àoyuán*	澳元
New Zealand dollar	*xīnxīlányuán*	新西兰元
Pound sterling	*yīngbàng*	英镑
Japanese yen	*rìyuán*	日元
Hong Kong dollar	*gǎngbì*	港币
Euro	*ōuyuán*	欧元

Key Words

currency	*bì*	币	mark	*mǎkè*	马克
dollar	*yuán*	元	peso	*bǐsuǒ*	比索
franc	*fǎláng*	法郎	pound	*bàng*	镑
lira	*lǐlā*	里拉	rupee	*lúbǐ*	卢比

208

Appendix F

Place Names

Major Administrative Divisions

China is divided into 23 provinces, 5 autonomous regions, 4 municipalities directly under the Central Government, and 2 special administrative regions.

Municipalities under the Central Government

北京	*Běijīng*
上海	*Shànghǎi*
天津	*Tiānjīn*
重庆	*Chóngqìng*

Autonomous Regions

广西	*Guǎngxī* (Zhuang Autonomous Region)
内蒙古	*Nèi Měnggǔ* (Inner Mongolia Autonomous Region)
宁夏	*Níngxià* (Hui Autonomous Region)
新疆	*Xīnjiāng* (Uygur Autonomous Region)
西藏	*Xīzàng* (Tibet Autonomous Region)

Provinces

安徽省	*Ānhuī*	江西	*Jiāngxī*
福建	*Fújiàn*	吉林	*Jílín*
甘肃	*Gānsù*	辽宁	*Liáoníng*
广东	*Guǎngdōng*	青海	*Qīnghǎi*
贵州	*Guìzhōu*	山东	*Shāndōng*
海南	*Hǎinán*	山西	*Shānxī*
河北	*Héběi*	陕西	*Shǎnxī*
河南	*Hénán*		(Shaanxi)
黑龙江	*Hēilóngjiāng*	四川	*Sìchuān*
湖北	*Húběi*	台湾	*Táiwān*
湖南	*Húnán*	云南	*Yúnnán*
江苏	*Jiāngsū*	浙江	*Zhèjiāng*

APPENDIX F

Special Administrative Regions

| 香港 | *Xiānggǎng* | (Hong Kong) |
| 澳门 | *Àomén* | (Macao) |

Cities of Interest

Below is a selected list of cities with historic, cultural, or economic significance.

鞍山	*Ānshān*	江陵	*Jiānglíng*
包头	*Bāotóu*	景德镇	*Jǐngdézhèn*
保定	*Bǎodìng*	景洪	*Jǐnghóng*
北戴河	*Běidàihé*	喀什	*Kāshí*
北京	*Běijīng*		(Kashgar)
长春	*Chángchūn*	开封	*Kāifēng*
长沙	*Chángshā*	昆明	*Kūnmíng*
承德	*Chéngdē*	拉萨	*Lāsà* (Lhasa)
成都	*Chéngdū*	兰州	*Lánzhōu*
重庆	*Chóngqìng*	洛阳	*Luòyáng*
大理	*Dàlǐ*	南昌	*Nánchāng*
大连	*Dàlián*	南京	*Nánjīng*
大同	*Dàtóng*	南宁	*Nánníng*
大足	*Dàzú*	宁波	*Níngbō*
敦煌	*Dūnhuáng*	青岛	*Qīngdǎo*
佛山	*Fóshān*	曲阜	*Qūfù*
抚顺	*Fǔshùn*	泉州	*Quánzhōu*
福州	*Fúzhōu*	日喀则	*Rìkezé*
格尔木	*Gé'ěrmù*		(Shigatse,
	(Golmud)		Xigaze)
广州	*Guǎngzhōu*	上海	*Shànghǎi*
	(Canton)	韶山	*Sháoshān*
桂林	*Guìlín*	绍兴	*Shàoxīng*
哈尔滨	*Hā'ěr bīn*	深圳	*Shēnzhèn*
	(Harbin)	沈阳	*Shěnyáng*
海口	*Hǎikǒu*	石家庄	*Shíjiāzhuāng*
杭州	*Hángzhōu*	苏州	*Sūzhōu*
合肥	*Héféi*	太原	*Tàiyuán*

呼和浩特	*Hūhéhàotè* (Hohhot)	天津	*Tiānjīn*
吉林	*Jílín*	吐鲁番	*Tǔlǔfān* (Turfan)
济南	*Jǐnán*	温州	*Wēnzhōu*
乌鲁木齐	*Wūlǔmùqí* (Urumqi)	延安	*Yán'ān*
无锡	*Wúxī*	扬州	*Yángzhōu*
武汉	*Wǔhàn*	宜昌	*Yíchāng*
西安	*Xī'ān*	岳阳	*Yuèyáng*
西宁	*Xīníng*	肇庆	*Zhàoqìng*
厦门	*Xiàmén* (Amoy)	镇江	*Zhènjiāng*
		郑州	*Zhèngzhōu*

Dynasties

The Chinese dynasties are outlined here in brief.

Xia 夏		2070 BC - 1600 BC
Shang 商		1600 BC - 1046 BC
Zhou 周		1046 BC - 256 BC
Western Zhou	西周	1046 BC - 771 BC
Eastern Zhou	东周	770 BC - 256 BC
Spring and Autumn	春秋	770 BC - 476 BC
Warring States	战国	475 BC - 221 BC
Qin 秦		221 BC - 206 BC
Han 汉		206 BC - 220AD
Western Han	西汉	206 BC - 25 AD
Eastern Han	东汉	25 - 220
Three Kingdoms	三国	220 - 280
Jin 晋		265 - 420
Western Jin	西晋	265 - 317
Eastern Jin	东晋	317 - 420
Northern and Southern Dynasties	南北朝	420 - 589
Sui 隋		581 - 618
Tang 唐		618 - 907
Five Dynasties	五代	907 - 960
Song 宋		960 - 1279
Northern Song	南宋	960 - 1127
Southern Song	北宋	1127 - 1279
Yuan 元		1279 - 1368
Ming 明		1368 - 1644
Qing 清		1644-1911

Appendix H

Family Relations

In Chinese, addressing relatives is not just a matter of calling "aunt" or "uncle"—you have to specify whether the relative is on your mother or father's side and sometimes the relative's age in respect to yourself or your parent.

Paternal Relatives

爷爷	yéye	grandfather
奶奶	nǎinai	grandmother
伯伯	bóbo	uncle (father's older brother)
伯母	bómǔ	his wife
叔叔	shūshu	uncle (father's younger brother)
婶婶	shěnshen	his wife
姑姑	gūgu	aunt (father's sister)
姑夫	gūfu	her husband
堂哥	tánggē	older boy cousin
堂弟	tángdì	younger boy cousin
堂姐	tángjiě	older girl cousin
堂妹	tángmèi	younger girl cousin

Maternal Relatives

姥爷,外公	lǎoye, wàigōng	grandfather
姥姥,外婆	lǎolao, wàipó	grandmother
姨姨	yíyi	aunt (mother's sister)
姨夫	yífu	her husband
舅舅	jiùjiu	uncle (mother's brother)
舅妈	jiùmā	his wife
表哥	biǎogē	older boy cousin
表弟	biǎodì	younger boy cousin
表姐	biǎojiě	older girl cousin
表妹	biǎomèi	younger girl cousin

Immediate Family

爸爸	bába	father
妈妈	māma	mother
哥哥	gēge	older brother
嫂子	sǎozi	his wife
弟弟	dìdi	younger brother
弟妹,弟媳	dìmèi, dìxí	his wife
姐姐	jiějie	older sister
姐夫	jiěfu	her husband
妹妹	mèimei	younger sister
妹夫	mèifu	her husband
女儿	nǚér	daughter
女婿	nǚxu	son-in-law
儿子	érzi	son
儿媳	érxí	daughter-in-law
孙子	sūnzi	grandson (son's son)
孙女	sūnnǚ	granddaughter (son's daughter)
外孙	wàisūn	grandson (daughter's son)
外孙女	wàisūnnǚ	granddaughter (daughter's daughter)

Appendix I

Useful Telephone Numbers

Emergency

Fire: 119
Police: 110
Traffic accident: 122
First Aid / Ambulance: 120
Beijing Public Security
    Bureau English Department: 84020101
International SOS Assistance: 64629100

Others

Local phone number inquiry: 114
Weather forecast: 12121
Speaking clock: 12117
International Phone Directory: 115
Beijing Customs: 65396114
Tourist Information: 65130828
Bus Hotline: 96166
Public Transport Superpass Hotline: 88087733
BCNC Car Rental Toll-free: 800-810-9001
Ticket Booking Hotline: 64177845 or 800-810-3721
Customer Complaint: 12315 or 96315

图书在版编目（CIP）数据

旅游会话／陈蒙惠，殷边编著．

北京：外文出版社，2007

ISBN 978-7-119-04792-8

I.旅… II.①陈…②殷… III.旅游－汉语－口语－对外汉语教学－教材
IV.H195.4

中国版本图书馆CIP数据核字（2007）第060289号

策划编辑：许　荣
责任编辑：严　晶
英文审定：许　荣
封面设计：何永妍
内文设计：楼德政
印刷监制：冯　浩

旅游会话

陈蒙惠，殷边　编著

©2007 陈蒙惠
出版发行：
外文出版社（中国北京百万庄大街24号）
邮政编码：100037
网址：http://www.flp.com.cn
电话：008610-68320579　（总编室）
　　　008610-68995852　（发行部）
　　　008610-68327750　（版权部）
制版：
北京维诺传媒文化有限公司
印刷：
北京蓝空印刷厂
开本：787mm×1092mm　1/36　印张：7.25
2008年第1版　第2次印刷
（英）
ISBN 978-7-119-04792-8
03500（平）
9-CE-3790P